Praise for *Web Services and Service-Oriented Architectures: The Savvy Manager's Guide*

"The new field of integration via Web Services, is, unfortunately, a hype minefield. It wouldn't surprise me to see a Web Services tool packaged with Ginzu knives! Doug Barry demystifies the new but burgeoning field with a refreshing business-oriented point of view. What drives adoption? What corporate forces will resist adoption? Most importantly, *The Savvy Manager's Guide* explains how all of this great new stuff is going to leverage existing infrastructure in real corporate settings, and benefit from modern software development processes like Model Driven Architecture. A great read!"

Richard Mark Soley, Ph.D.
Chairman and CEO, Object Management Group, Inc.

"While there are a number of good Web services books aimed at developers, there has been a peculiar lack of books that deal with the very real and important issues that IT managers have to face in order to assess and implement Web services in their organizations. In this respect, Doug Barry's book is a very welcome addition to the Web services literature. Although all the important technical details are very well covered with very clear and insightful analogies, the most valuable aspects of this book are the chapters that cover Web services from a manager's perspective. For example, the discussion on the common beliefs about enterprise architectures and how they relate to Web services is a gem and worth the price of the book. Similarly insightful chapters cover the impact of Web services on the enterprise, adoption steps and change management issues in implementing Web services projects. This a great book that every manager contemplating a Web services project should read."

Toufic Boubez, Ph.D.
Chief Technology Officer, Layer-7 Software
Coauthor of *Building Web Services with Java: Making Sense of XML, SOAP, WSDL and UDDI*

"Douglas Barry has provided a solid description of what are web services, how they can be used, how they are developed and what they are based on. His background work for many years with technology standards consortiums enables him to clearly show why the widespread adoption of web services is closely tied to the agreed use of common standard vocabularies and methods for inter-enterprise interactions.

The book is an easy read for managers, both business and technology managers, with clear example usage scenarios, extensive references and practical implementation guidelines.

Douglas Barry paints a clear picture of a future world where services are ubiquitous and easily integrated into the way we w   it is easily within our grasps. But it will be a worl   mation change their thinking to a more service   chnology features are implemented within indus   g repeat- edly points out, 'Of course, for this to   n of the types of messages and data exchanges r

Patrick Gannon
President and CEO, OASIS

D1367613

The Savvy Manager's Guides
Series Editor, Douglas K. Barry

Web Services and Service-Oriented Architectures
Douglas K. Barry

Forthcoming

Semantics in Business Systems
Dave McComb

Business Intelligence
David Loshin

Web Services and Service-Oriented Architectures

THE SAVVY MANAGER'S GUIDE

➤ | *Your Road Map to Emerging IT*

Douglas K. Barry

MORGAN KAUFMANN PUBLISHERS

An Imprint of Elsevier

AMSTERDAM   BOSTON   LONDON   NEW YORK
OXFORD   PARIS   SAN DIEGO   SAN FRANCISCO
SINGAPORE   SYDNEY   TOKYO

Senior Editor	Lothlórien Homet
Publishing Services Manager	Simon Crump
Editorial Assistant	Corina Derman
Project Management	Graphic World Publishing Services
Cover Design	Frances Baca Design
Cover Image	Color Day Production / Getty Images
Text Design	Frances Baca Design
Technical Illustration	Technologies 'N Typography
Composition	Nancy Logan
Copyeditor	Graphic World Publishing Services
Proofreader	Graphic World Publishing Services
Indexer	Steve Rath
Printer	The Maple-Vail Book Manufacturing Group

Designations used by companies to distinguish their products are often claimed as trademarks or registered trademarks. In all instances in which Morgan Kaufmann Publishers is aware of a claim, the product names appear in initial capital or all capital letters. Readers, however, should contact the appropriate companies for more complete information regarding trademarks and registration.

Morgan Kaufmann Publishers
An Imprint of Elsevier
340 Pine Street, Sixth Floor
San Francisco, CA 94104-3205
www.mkp.com

07 06 05 04   5 4 3

Library of Congress Control Number: 2002116250
ISBN: 1-55860-906-7

This book is printed on acid-free paper.

Foreword

Picture a world where services are ubiquitous and organically integrated into the way we think and work. A place where both users and providers of information interact through a common focus on services. A world where technology is implemented within industry frameworks that operate on a global scale, enabled by open, interoperable standards.

To some, this vision may seem impossible to realize or at the very least, a long way off. However, those who follow the evolution of information and communications technology appreciate that the dream is quite surely within our grasp. Indeed, the widespread benefits of Web services are easily achievable within the next two to five years.

Douglas Barry's *Web Services and Service-Oriented Architectures: The Savvy Manager's Guide* provides both a road map and a how-to guide for transforming the possible into the actual. The book delivers a solid description of what Web services are, how they can be used, how service-oriented architectures are developed, and some detailed options for successful implementation.

Readers will find very practical steps to guide them in planning and justifying the use of Web services. The following summary statement provides insight into the business-oriented approach the author takes to explain the expected benefits. "Service-oriented architectures that use Web services will result in a blurring between internal and external services. Architectures will be constructed using a combination of those internal and external services. As time goes on, these services will become more standardized making it easier to replace one 'plug-compatible' service with another. The result will be competition to create higher quality software in these services."

It is important to appreciate, however, that two fundamental issues must be addressed before we can herald the brave, new world Barry describes.

A common framework for Web service interactions based on open standards must occur.

An agreed set of vocabularies and interactions for specific industries or common functions must be adopted.

A common framework is essential to provide a sustainable foundation that will allow end-user companies to achieve the payback they require to invest widely in the service-oriented architecture. An interview with the CIO of a Fortune 50 corporation in 2003 provided this response to a question about his greatest concern over adoption of Web services.

"One is fragmentation. There's a sordid history in the technology world of everybody trying to get a little leverage over somebody else by developing proprietary extensions or vendor-specific add-ons to the core technology. In general, those have been bad, because they don't end up being sustainable over time and that costs companies like us a lot of money."

The second highest priority that must be achieved is standard, open vocabularies and interactions (transactions). As Barry repeatedly points out, "Of course, for this [service-oriented scenario] to happen, there needs to be standardization of the types of messages and data exchanges needed with a CRM system." Barry provides multiple examples of the type of standardization that must be realized in order for the scenarios depicted to be carried out seamlessly and efficiently.

The real meat of Barry's perspective is found in Part II—Managing Change Needed for a Service-Oriented Architecture. Here, Barry brings together interrelated issues for the organization, technology and the people involved in deploying service-oriented architecture. He also delves into the change options related to database systems, message routers, internal applications and the various architectural options.

Web Services and Service-Oriented Architectures: The Savvy Manager's Guide gives business managers much-needed help in assessing the costs and benefits of adopting Web services standards and building their own service-oriented architectures. Barry's many years of work with technology standards consortia enables him to clearly explain why the widespread adoption of Web services is closely tied to the agreed use of common standard vocabularies and methods for inter-enterprise transactions.

What will happen if Web services standards and common vocabularies are not developed and implemented in the near term? Certainly, the benefits of service-oriented architectures as outlined by Barry will be delayed or restricted to a few specialized areas or a handful of proprietary vendor installations. Software providers, seeking widespread markets for their Web service tools and application development platforms, won't be the only ones at risk. I contend that that the negative impact will be even more pervasive, and the biggest fallout will be felt by end-user companies, unable to achieve the cost reduction and service expansion benefits that a widespread deployment of standards-based Web services would enable. In this post-dot-com era, end user companies are expecting more liquidity and longevity of their assets. If they are unable to achieve the expected benefits, they will likely abandon the technology as just another over-hyped promise of software vendors.

Clearly, the time to forge a common framework based on interoperable standards and open vocabularies is now. *Web Services and Service-Oriented Architectures: The Savvy Manager's Guide* puts these requirements into context and gives readers the information they need to advance this development and assure that the promises of Web services remain within reach.

Patrick J. Gannon
President & CEO
OASIS

Contents

Introduction

One of the toughest jobs for managers today is keeping up with the rapid changes in technology. The advent of Web Services and service-oriented architectures makes this more important, because these technologies are going to fundamentally change the way we build our internal systems—the information systems that support our organizations—and how our internal systems interact with external systems. There has been nothing like this before in the software industry. We are on the cusp of building "plug-compatible" software components that will reduce the costs of our software systems at the same time increasing the capabilities of the systems. Sure, you have heard that promise more than once before. And more than once, the delivery fell short of the promise. But, as with such promises, they will come true some day. That time is now.

This is a guide for the savvy manager who wants to capitalize on the wave of change that will occur with Web Services and service-oriented architectures. The changes wrought by this technology will require both a grasp of the technology and a way to deal with how these changes will affect the people who build our systems in our organizations. This book covers both issues. Managers at all levels of all organizations must be aware of the changes that are on the horizon and ways to deal with both sets of issues.

This is a nontechnical book on a technical subject. It assumes no prior knowledge of the technology. It is written with a high-level view at the beginning of the book. As the book progresses, technical details are introduced and explained. You can keep reading until you have enough understanding of the technology for your use. If you read through to Part III, you will see some architectural options that you might consider when using Web Services and service-oriented architectures. Part IV serves as a reference guide for the buzzwords and acronyms associated with this technology.

This book does not define a new methodology. Instead, it shows how aspects of a service-oriented architecture augment or are compatible with most software architecture methodologies and frameworks.

The intent of this book is to give you an opportunity to consider some ideas and advice that just might make it easier for your organization to realize the potential benefits in Web Services and service-oriented architectures.

Business Opportunities Addressed

Web Services and service-oriented architectures can:

- Expand your information technology options
- Make your information technology systems more flexible and responsive
- Reduce development time
- Reduce maintenance costs.

This book will make the case for why these promises will be fulfilled this time. Read through to the end of Part II to see why this technology will eliminate most technological barriers to creating "plug-compatible" software and why the biggest challenge for managers is handling the people issues related to this change.

Structure of This Book

Part I (Chapters 1 through 7) begins with a high-level example of how an average person in an organization might interact with a service-oriented architecture based on Web Services. Each of the technologies is then explained in more detail. As Part I progresses, technical detail is added in a "peeling of the onion" approach. Forces affecting the adoption of Web Services and other integration techniques are analyzed. The growing impact of Web Services is explored along with beliefs about enterprise architectures. Part I ends with the stages of adoption for service-oriented architectures.

Part II (Chapters 8 and 9) deals with managing change needed for a service-oriented architecture. Because the potential change related to service-oriented architectures will likely be far reaching in our organizations, management of this change is critical. This part discusses resistance to change, provides suggestions on how to overcome resistance, and provides tips for managing change issues during the development of service-oriented architectures. Although resistance to change is a huge issue to which whole books have been dedicated, the approach here is to look specifically at resistance issues related to technology acceptance.

Part III (Chapters 10 through 13) outlines the "nuts and bolts" of creating a service-oriented architecture. It provides possible architectures at each stage of adoption for Web Services along an analysis of various architectural options.

Part IV (Chapters 14 and 15) is a compendium of software technology and terminology related to Web Services and service-oriented architectures. This makes for a quick reference guide.

Service-Oriented Architecture Overview

The future of software will involve some type of service-oriented architecture; this is an assumption in this book. With such an architecture, we will see more packaged software—used either as an internal service or an external service—available over the Internet. We will connect these services together to create the information technology systems of the future. These systems will require less custom software in organizations and more creativity in the connections between the services. This is a natural evolution of software technology and will be explained further in this book.

No crystal ball exists to tell us the services that will be available. Undoubtedly, there will many innovative services that we cannot envision at this time. For that reason, this book presents relatively straightforward data-centric and distributed process approaches that will help you get your organization ready to take advantage of a service-oriented architecture—in whatever form it takes.

The first part of this book begins with a story that illustrates how a service-oriented architecture and Web Services might be used for planning and taking a business trip in the not-too-distant future. Following the story, the next chapter outlines a high-level explanation of the technology and related standards involved in this trip. That leads to the introduction of service-oriented architectures and Web Services in Chapter 3. This chapter also introduces an important premise of this book: that adopting this technology will bring radical change to our systems and organizations. In Chapter 4, forces affecting the adoption of Web Services and other system integration techniques are analyzed, along with an overview of how the impact of Web Services will change over time. In Chapter 5, the focus shifts to a description of the growing impact of Web Services. The impact will likely start in small, simple efforts and grow to involve enterprise architectures and business-to-business applications. Chapter 6 covers beliefs and issues with enterprise architectural efforts and shows the advantages of using a service-oriented architecture within a wider enterprise architecture. The final chapter of Part I introduces steps in starting to adopt a service-oriented architecture along with a vision for the future of our information technology organizations.

CHAPTER 1

A Business Trip in the Not-Too-Distant Future

This chapter is a story of a business trip that illustrates how a service-oriented architecture and Web Services might be used in the not-too-distant future. It provides a vision of how a service-oriented architecture might work in an organization.

> ➤ The term *Web Services* can be confusing. It is, unfortunately, often used in many different ways. Compounding this confusion is the term *services,* which has a different meaning than the term *Web Services*. In this book, the term *Web Services* refers to the technologies that allow for making connections. Services are what you connect together using Web Services. A service is the endpoint of a connection. Also, a service has some type of underlying computer system that supports the connection offered. The combination of services—internal and external to an organization—make up a *service-oriented architecture*. A term less commonly used is *composite application*. A composite application is created by combining services. Composite applications are built using a service-oriented architecture.

The Business Trip

This is the story of C. R. C. R. is short for Connected Representative. C. R. is about to take a business trip that will occur in the not-too-distant future. This trip is much like any business trip. It will involve flying to California from the Midwest, renting a car, and visiting several customers in different cities over 3 or 4 days.

To start his trip planning, C. R. uses his browser to see all the possible customers he could visit within driving distance of his destination city.

Although there are a few customers he knows that he wants to visit, he also wants to make sure he is keeping in touch with as many customers as he can. Using his browser, he selects the three customers that he must visit. C. R. sorts the remaining customers by the number of problems reported in the previous 3 months and by the revenue C. R.'s organization has received from these customers. Using this list, he identifies ten additional customers he might see and they are listed in order of importance according to his chosen criteria. C. R. adds the dates he wants to leave and return and selects the "Submit" button and moves on to working on other things.

A little while later, C. R. receives an e-mail message from his contact at one of the customers saying that dinner on Tuesday would be great, but the customer would need to meet an hour later than C. R. suggested. C. R. opens up his calendar on his browser and adjusts the dinner time already on his calendar and replies to the e-mail message.

> *I am going depart from the story here for a moment. You will note that C. R. did not originally set up the dinner time. This was done for him by the software system. We see how this was done later in this book.*

As the day progresses, C. R. gets a few more e-mail messages and he updates his calendar accordingly. Within a few hours, he also receives information on his flights, car rental, and hotel reservations at three cities. C. R. again opens up his calendar on his browser just to check that everything looks okay. The arrangements are fine and he confirms the plans. At this point, his manager receives basic information about C. R.'s trip along with notes on her calendar about when he departs and returns. C. R.'s spouse also receives updates to her calendar that include the departure and return trips along with the hotels where C. R. will be staying and hotel phone numbers inserted in the appropriate days. This is something she likes to have handy when C. R. is traveling.

The day before his trip, C. R. downloads what he needs to his cellular telephone/palmtop computer. This includes the itinerary showing his flights, car reservation, hotel reservations, hotel contact information, details on each customer, a summary of all contacts C. R.'s organization has had with each customer, driving instructions from each stop along the way, and maps. C. R. prints out the driving instructions and maps. He likes to have paper copies just in case his rental car does not have a Global Positioning System (GPS) driving assistant or the GPS doesn't work properly. C. R. thinks it's always nice to have a paper map and driving instructions.

When C. R. arrives at his destination airport, he is pleased to see that his rental car has the GPS assistant that his car rental profile requests. He starts the car, and the GPS assistant is already programmed for his first destination that day—one of the customer sites. C. R.'s organization recently switched to this car rental company because they offered this feature. It beats having to punch in destination addresses every time.

> ➤ *In this story, it was relatively recently that rental companies agreed on the data and the names to use when describing the data used to transmit itineraries for GPS assistants. C. R.'s organization switched to the new rental company because of this feature, because the new company provided almost the same rates as their previous car rental company.*

On his way to his first customer visit, C. R. receives an instant text message on his cellular telephone indicating that someone at this customer just reported a significant problem with one of the products from C. R.'s organization. This is good to know before going into his first meeting. While in the customer's parking lot before the meeting, C. R. calls the representative who is working on the problem for any additional information before heading into his meeting. C. R. was able to address his customer's concerns on the spot.

Back out at the parking lot, C. R. sees that he has another instant message telling him that his itinerary has changed on the third day and that he should check his calendar. He takes out his palmtop and logs onto his online calendar, downloading what he needs. He sees that the last customer he wanted to see has canceled (an e-mail message explains why) and that two different customers were added to his trip. This change also necessitated changing hotels. Thankfully, C. R.'s spouse and manager also received the updates to their calendars automatically. The hotel reservations have been changed appropriately, too. When C. R. started his car the following morning, the updated itinerary was also downloaded to his car's GPS assistant.

Late that night, C. R. was looking over the customer visits for the next day and saw something puzzling in the summary of contacts for one of the customers. For some reason, the same problem appeared to be reported multiple times. He used the monitor and keyboard in his hotel room to get more information on this contact from the online repository that contained all contact information for his organization.

As C. R. meets with customers, he makes notes on his palmtop about each of the meetings. At intervals, his palmtop transmits that meeting contact information and it is added to all the other contact information for each of the customers.

> ➤ | *By now, you have probably noticed that C. R.'s organization has very current and detailed information on every customer contact. They found that in their industry, this makes a big difference in how well the employees can help their customers. It also identifies any need that the customer may have for additional products or services. This customer information comes from multiple sources, both internal and external to C. R.'s organization.*

On the last day of his trip, C. R. receives an instant message in the morning that his flight that afternoon has been cancelled, but that the airline has arranged an alternate flight that will leave an hour later. C. R.'s spouse also receives an instant message with the same information. Both of their online calendars were updated to reflect the new arrival time that evening. C. R. also used his palmtop to check any last minute flight changes with his airline.

Summary

A lot of technology is involved behind the scenes in this story. Also, there obviously needs to be agreements and standards among organizations to make this level of data interchange possible. This technology and the standards make it possible for C. R. to be "connected" on his business trip. The next chapter provides a high-level explanation of the technology and standards that made this possible.

Information Technology Used in This Trip

Chapter 2 provides a high-level explanation of the technology and standards used in the business trip described in the previous chapter. Many services and supporting technologies came together in the business trip story. These include online repositories, customer relationship management, online calendar services, travel agencies, car rental, and more. We examine each of these in this chapter. As you read this chapter, note that it is relatively easy to swap out one service provider for another. This is because of standards related to data interchange. The result, as shown in this story, is that competition is related to either cost or innovation.

In this story, there is a tremendous amount of technology and data interchange going on behind the scene. Let's look at some of the information technology used. Figure 2.1 shows the ways in which the various services exchanged data in this story. The following sections of this chapter provide more information on the services and data interchange shown in this figure.

Keeping Track of All Customer Contacts in an Online Repository

Remember that C. R.'s organization decided it was important to keep track of all customer contacts. They did this by using an online repository.[1] This repository is behind their firewall and is served by a cluster of application servers. Both the application servers and repository are also *fault tolerant*. This means

---

1. For the purposes of this story and figure, the term "repository" is used. In reality, this could easily be a collection of databases and it also might entail routing data to multiple locations. Data routing will be covered in Chapter 4.

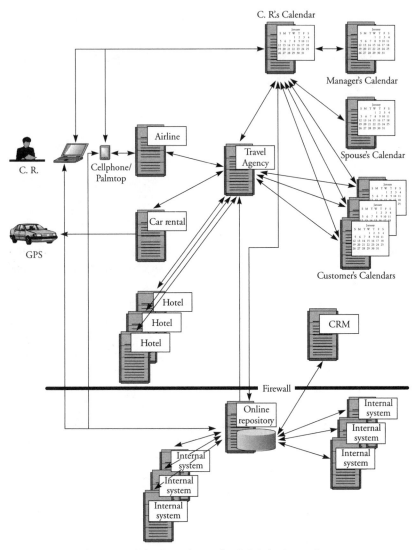

FIGURE 2.1 Services and data interchange for C. R.'s business trip.

that they are capable of being accessible virtually all the time even when there are hardware and software failures. The application servers and repository are fault tolerant because the wide, internal use of customer contact data requires that they be accessible all the time.

C. R.'s organization did not always have data in one place. At one time, some customer contact information was in their Customer Relationship

Management (CRM) system, some in the accounting system, and still more was scattered in other internal systems and in such places as the representative personal records and in trip reports.

C. R.'s organization had to decide what data should be in their online repository and develop such things as naming conventions and the meaning of each item of data. Fortunately, because of his organization's work in Electronic Data Interchange (EDI) and Web Services, a fair number of data elements were already established.[2]

Using this online repository along with a business intelligence (BI) package, allowed C. R. to determine which customers would be best for him to visit. The BI package also can be used to identify various patterns in customer contacts and purchases.

Once the repository was established, it became relatively easy to use Web Services to connect to various online calendar services. For example, C. R.'s online calendar service used Web Services to automatically add the customer contacts made during the business trip. This illustrates a *data-centric approach* that will be discussed further in Part III. (It is a data-centric approach because it is based on moving data to where the data might be needed.)

Obtaining Company Contact Information from an External CRM Service

By creating a separate online repository, C. R.'s organization also found it relatively easy to move from one CRM product to another when a new service provides more CRM features or a better price. This was possible because the data from the old, internal CRM product was transmitted via Web Services to the repository. Changing to a new CRM product meant the same data could be transmitted, but in this case from the new, external CRM service.

 Of course, for this to happen, there needed to be standardization of the types of messages and data exchanges needed with a CRM system. For the sake of this story, we will assume that industry consortia were able to develop those standards. Information on industry consortia can be found on page 191.

Actually, C. R. did not know that the CRM his organization currently uses is provided as an outside service and was no longer behind his organization's firewall. It didn't matter to him, except that it seemed to be working

---

2. Work on standards will be discussed later in this book. If you want to see a sampling of standards efforts by industry, a listing starts on page 191.

fine. It did matter to his organization, though. As it turned out, the organization changed to an external CRM because the external service had a much better user interface and could be used with a monthly service charge instead of buying an upgrade to the aging, internal CRM product. The only requirement for the switch was that the new CRM service could provide the same data over Web Services to the repository as the old CRM product. Because an industry standards body had standardized most of that data, this was no problem. In fact, the new CRM service sends more data than is needed. But because the data is sent as XML (see page 209), the extra data isn't used for the online repository. There is no problem receiving the extra data.[3]

Online Calendar Services

There were multiple online calendars involved in the example of C. R.'s business trip:

- C. R.'s calendar
- C. R.'s spouse's calendar
- C. R.'s manager's calendar
- The calendar for each customer visited.

Just to make it more complicated, let's say each calendar is maintained by a different online service. They communicate with each other using Web Services and a standard set of data elements.

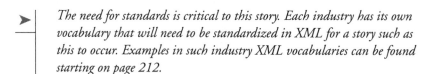

The need for standards is critical to this story. Each industry has its own vocabulary that will need to be standardized in XML for a story such as this to occur. Examples in such industry XML vocabularies can be found starting on page 212.

C. R. has established a set of rules for business trips. These rules indicate what details about a trip will be sent to his manager's calendar, his spouse's calendar, each customer's calendar, and to the online repository his organization maintains.

Each of the online calendars that receives information from C. R.'s calendar has a set of rules about what types of updates they will accept. Often, *agent* software enforces these rules. Software agents can use rules to monitor

---

3. As will be shown later, XML uses a structure that effectively makes the messages longer. The longer messages may present a problem for some highly time-critical applications. Nevertheless, for the majority of uses, advances in transmittal speeds more than offset the extra time needed to transmit XML messages.

changes and report those changes using Web Services (see page 164). For example, a customer's calendar agent will respond whether or not a specific time and date is a good time for a one-hour meeting with C. R. The customer's calendar, however, won't disclose information about other items on the customer's schedule to C. R.'s calendar.

Online calendars are most likely to communicate with other software agents. These could include travel, airline, and hotel software agents.

Changing from One Online Calendar Service to Another

C. R. found that he has been changing calendar services frequently lately. He started out using one provided by his organization, but because of the standardization of data interchange, several companies have found it possible to lure people to change calendar services using price or other feature incentives. In C. R.'s case, he has switched primarily because he prefers specific features that are offered. One that he particularly likes is the ability to set up rules to automatically perform functions such as informing his spouse of his schedule changes.

The standardization of data interchange makes most of the changes easy to do. C. R. does, however, still need to create a traveler profile each time he switches services. In part, the calendar services compete on the capabilities of the profiles now that they all exchange data with other calendar services and other external services in the same way.

One real time saver that C. R.'s organization added when the calendar data interchange standard became available was the ability to accept data from calendar services for their online repository. This is how C. R. was able to add contact information automatically from his business trip from his calendar service to the online repository. C. R.'s organization can accept such information from any calendar service that uses the standard data interchange.[4]

Getting Updates on Clients to Be Visited While on the Road

One feature C. R. particularly likes about his calendar service is the ability to set up rules that determine how he is informed of changes to his schedule. For

---

4. Security is obviously an important concern with using Web Services. Information on security can be found on page 32.

example, he has established a rule that any changes that occur within 5 days of a customer meeting will be sent to his cellular telephone via instant text messaging. He could have had a voice message or e-mail message, but C. R. prefers the instant messages.

For C. R. to receive the instant message concerning a very recent problem that a customer had, the online repository must have updated C. R.'s calendar in some way. Standardization of data interchange for calendar services makes this possible. There was a time after C. R.'s organization had set up the online repository when the standardization of calendar data interchange had not yet occurred. Back then, C. R. had to log into the repository the night before each customer visit to check to see if anything had been recorded recently. Getting the instant messages saves a lot of time and, in the case of our story, gave C. R. last minute information about a problem encountered by the customer he was about to visit.

Travel Agency Service

The travel agency that C. R. uses is a service external to his organization. It is entirely automated. C. R. has a travel profile that covers the usual items such as preferred airline seating, rental car (with a GPS assistant), preferred hotels, and so on. It also contains rules about updating C. R.'s calendar and the other calendars mentioned.

When setting up his trip, C. R. used the online repository to select both priority customers and those that would be nice to visit. The necessary contact information was sent to the travel agent from the repository when C. R. pressed the "Submit" button.

This travel agent can interact with the software agents that handle the calendars. In the story, there was one e-mail message that the travel agent could not handle concerning the change in a dinner time. That e-mail message was passed along to C. R. When he looked at his online calendar to make the change in the dinner date, he also saw the other arrangements already made for him by his automated travel agent.

C. R.'s travel agent also sent the travel information to the car rental company using Web Services. In turn, the rental company transmitted the itinerary to the GPS assistant in his car. Some other systems might allow beaming an itinerary from a palmtop to the GPS assistant in the car.

Finally, while C. R. was on the road, one of his customers cancelled. This software travel agent contacted other names that C. R. had originally provided and arranged new meetings, changed the hotel reservations, and informed both C. R.'s spouse's calendar and his manager's calendar of the change.

A characteristic of the travel service agent is that it always needs the latest information from multiple sources. This illustrates the *distributed-process* approach that will be discussed further in Part III. It is a distributed-process approach because the service depends on having the latest information *processed* at multiple locations *distributed* through an Intranet or on the Internet.

Car Rental Service

In our story, C. R. liked using a GPS assistant when driving on business trips. The travel agent service can send the car rental service the necessary information so that an itinerary can be downloaded from the satellite at any time. This is how the GPS assistant in C. R.'s car received the updated itinerary. It also illustrates how Web Services can be extended to all sorts of systems and not just application servers or enterprise-level systems.

Airlines and Hotel

Data interchange standardization is an important theme in this story and in the future of the technology used in organizations. The airlines and hotels in this story used data interchange standards as well. This includes allowing C. R. to check the status of his flights from his palmtop. At one point, each airline had a proprietary way to check this information. Standardization of such data interchange made it possible for palmtops and cellular telephones to bundle the capability to check flight status in with their product.

Services as Commodities

As you may have noticed, some services in this story are treated as commodities:

- The CRM service replaced an internal service
- C. R. changed calendar services frequently
- C. R.'s organization recently switched car rental companies.

In the story, all these services provided some type of innovation beyond the basic, standard interchange of data. This innovation is where some organizations will compete using Web Services. Others will compete on providing just the basics at a lower cost.

Summary

Each of the services described in this chapter are part of a larger service-oriented architecture that uses Web Services. In fact, it is the assembly of such services that makes a service-oriented architecture. An important idea in this chapter is that it will become relatively easy to swap out one service provider for another. This is because of the XML-based standards that are being developed in various industry consortia. A second important idea is that Web Services will cause many services to be seen as commodities. This will result in competition in either cost or innovation within the standards. The next chapter will explain service-oriented architectures and Web Services.

CHAPTER 3

Service-Oriented Architectures and Web Services

Service-oriented architectures are all about connections. This chapter describes those connections. It begins with an analogy to connections used in audio-video (AV) systems (specifically, services in a service-oriented architecture are to AV components as Web Services are to the connections between AV components). Service-oriented architectures then are explained in more detail. This is followed by a description of ways that organizations of any size can use a service-oriented architecture and why most organizations likely will experience a blurring of internal and external services. Then Web Services are explained along with the use of XML. (Web Services using XML are the most common connections in a service-oriented architecture.[1]) The chapter wraps up with a summary of the security and authorization specifications related to Web Services.

➤ More often than not, you can look to the past to find a pattern that will allow you to predict the future. I had an epiphany of this sort concerning the future of software systems architecture when recently upgrading my AV system. The past in this case is the evolution of AV systems.

My AV system has components that have been purchased over the years. I wanted to add a DVD player to my system. The system has the usual cable box, receiver, VCR, CD player, speakers, and television set. One of the oldest components is the receiver and the DVD had connections that the receiver could not handle, such as s-video and optical connections. It did, however,

---

1. According to the W3C Web Services Architecture Work Group, a Web Service by definition uses XML. Although, in practice, there are exceptions. See page 30.

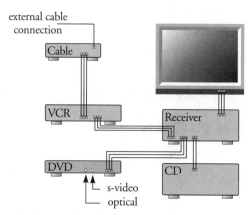

FIGURE 3.1 Audio-visual components.

have the common three RCA connections. I decided at that point to upgrade all of the connections in my AV system to RCA connections.[2]

Figure 3.1 shows how I connected the components after adding the DVD. These components could be connected in different ways, depending on what you want to do. For example, you could set up your cable connection to go through your VCR or split the signal so that you can watch one program and record another.

Not long ago, we had monolithic hi-fi or stereo systems. Then the industry settled on the various components in a stereo system and later video was added. What does this have to do with software systems architecture? Well, it's all in the connections. Web Services have provided an infrastructure for creating connections not unlike those we have with AV systems. And, just like AV systems, we will be able to assemble components in all sorts of ways because of those connections.

Service-Oriented Architecture Explained

The business trip that C. R. took in the introductory story involved using multiple services, both inside and outside his organization, such as travel agency, online calendar, or CRM services. From a software architectural

---

2. Serious audiophiles will probably point out that an RCA connector is not necessarily the highest performing option available. In fact, that is why RCA connectors make for a good analogy to using XML in Web Services. XML is also not the highest performing connection available. Nevertheless, much like an RCA connector, XML is undergoing standardization in ways that using it for data connections will be as ubiquitous as the RCA connectors.

point-of-view, this is a *service-oriented architecture.* A service-oriented architecture is essentially a collection of services. These services communicate with each other. The communication can involve either simple data passing or it could involve two or more services coordinating some activity. Some means of connecting services to each other is needed. Those connections are *Web Services.*

Services

If a service-oriented architecture is to be effective, we need a clear understanding of the term *service.* A service is a function that is well-defined, self-contained, and does not depend on the context or state of other services. Over time, the industry will standardize on the capabilities of various services.

The analogy to AV components fits well here. Each is well defined: the industry has decided what are the basic functions of a DVD player, a VCR, and so on. Each AV component is self-contained; you do not need a VCR, for example, to use a CD player. Finally, one AV component does not depend on another component. For example, the television does not need to be on to record using the VCR. True, if you play the recorded tape, you cannot see what is being played when the television is not turned on. Nevertheless, the VCR still does not need to know the context or state of the television.

The industry will define standard capabilities of CRM, Enterprise Resource Planning (ERP), and other services. These will become standard services and could, in some ways, be seen as commodities.[3] We may see these services come in various forms just as we see in buying AV components today. You can buy a DVD player bundled with a VCR or buy each component separately. Nevertheless, over the next few years, the industry will standardize the capabilities of various services much like the AV industry has standardized its components.[4]

What does this mean for software development? It means fewer people writing software and more organizations buying software rather the building it. Continuing with the AV analogy: I am old enough to have built my share of Heathkit electronics products for audio and other systems. (This was much like building your own software.) But the Heathkit era for electronics is over. Yes, I believe a lot of software development will go the same way.

---

3. As mentioned previously, the standardization of services will see competition in price or innovation. Continuing with the AV analogy, this commodity approach is what we see with various AV components—competition on either price or higher-end features.

4. The industry bodies working on standards and the various standards can be found in Chapter 14.

Connections

The technology of Web Services is being presented as the connection technology of the future. That is probably a fair assessment. Web Services essentially use XML to create a robust connection. The use of XML moves us away from the fragility of fixed record layout connections that can fail if proper formats are not used. XML also allows for the sending of more data than might be used. With Web Services, the extra data will not cause a problem with the receiving service.

Also, other existing connections are in use right now that won't go away for some time. These include the EDI standards, CORBA, and DCOM to name a few.[5] Again, much like the connections in AV systems, we can mix and match these connections and upgrade when it makes sense.

Connections such as Web Services are part of the inevitable evolution of interconnectedness. Consider how we can now exchange e-mail among disparate products. Although we could not do that at one time, we now take it for granted. This e-mail exchange is possible because of standards. Connections like Web Services (or the equivalent) will also be taken for granted some day because sets of standards will be developed.[6]

Figure 3.2 illustrates a basic service-oriented architecture. It shows a service consumer at the right sending a service request message to a service provider at the left. The service provider returns a response message to the service consumer. The request and subsequent response connections are defined in some way that is understandable to both the service consumer and service provider. How those connections are defined will be explained later in this chapter in the section that explains Web Services. A service provider can also be a service consumer. In the story of C. R.'s business trip, most of the service

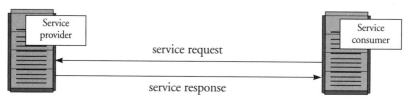

FIGURE 3.2 Service-oriented architecture basics.

---

5. EDI will be explained starting on page 65. CORBA and DCOM will be explained starting on page 45.

6. The organizations working on the standards can be found starting on page 191. Also, be sure to also see the sampling of standard XML vocabularies starting on page 212. Many industry groups are creating XML vocabularies specific to their industry.

providers were also service consumers. For example, the travel agency service provided travel information, but to do that it needed to consume information from hotel services, car rental services, and calendar services.

Organizations of Any Size Can Use a Service-Oriented Architecture

The use of a service-oriented architecture is not limited to large organizations. In fact, this architecture represents an opportunity for small and medium-sized organizations. Many services will be provided on some type of fee-for-use basis, which will make them economical for organizations of most any size. Other services might be provided at no cost. In the example of C. R.'s business trip, the travel agent service might charge for each use, whereas the external CRM service might charge a monthly fee for a certain number of users and the car rental and hotel services might be free.

The receipt of invoices illustrates a simple example of how a small business might benefit from a service. Right now, many invoices come in by mail or via fax. A service could be created that receives invoices using Web Services. The invoices might be held by the service until the accounting system that resides on the user's PC connects to receive the invoices—again, using Web Services. The invoices would then automatically update the accounting system on the PC. The analogy here would be to automated fax systems that currently exist to receive faxes which can, in turn, be downloaded to a fax machine at a later time. In this way, any organization, regardless of size, could take advantage of services for receiving invoices, making travel plans, coordinating calendars, trading commodities, and so on.

Blurring of Internal and External Services

In a service-oriented architecture, the distinction between internal and external services will become less apparent. In our story, C. R.'s organization changed from an aging internal CRM product to an external CRM service because the external service was more economical and had a better user interface. Because, in this story, all CRM services provide similar connections, changing from one service to another is not that major a change. (Much like swapping out one AV component for a new model. It might require upgrading some connections, but it is a relatively minor headache for the benefits.)

This will create a dynamic environment where software vendors will compete using features or innovations that are independent of the connections. This could include user interfaces, automated software agents, rule-based systems, or user profiles that allow for highly customized interactions.

Such market forces will affect internal development as well. It will be difficult for an internal development group in some organizations to compete with a software vendor that can recoup development costs by having many more customers than any internal development organization could imagine. The external vendor can achieve better product at a lower cost because of specialization. Internal development organizations will therefore shift to doing less development. The emphasis internally will shift to making all the connections work properly and integrating new services that might give an organization a competitive edge. An organization might also decide to provide a unique service that can be sold to other organizations.

Of course, organizations will only buy vendor-provided products and services if the software is of sufficient quality. Sometimes the reason why an organization develops its own software is that it experienced poor quality, vendor-provided software. Vendors planning to compete in this environment will need to be prepared to provide very high-quality software and a high level of customer service. Being able to treat services as commodities will allow an organization to switch services easily if it perceives either that the quality of software is poor or that they are not receiving sufficient support on any software-related issues.

Web Services Explained

Earlier, Web Services were described as the connection technology of the future. The remainder of this chapter is devoted to explaining Web Services. First, defining Web Services using Web Services Description Language (WSDL) will be reviewed. That will be followed by SOAP, which provides means of sending messages. As part of the explanation, XML tagged message formats will be compared to fixed record message formats to show the resilience of XML as part of a Web Services. Of course, XML is not the only option. The end of this section will cover options besides XML for Web Services.

Using the Web Services Description Language (WSDL)

WSDL forms the basis for Web Services. Figure 3.3 illustrates the use of WSDL. At the left is a service provider. At the right is a service consumer. The steps involved in providing and consuming a service are:

1. A service provider describes its service using WSDL. This definition is published to a directory of services. The directory could use Universal Description, Discovery, and Integration (UDDI). Other forms of directories can also be used.

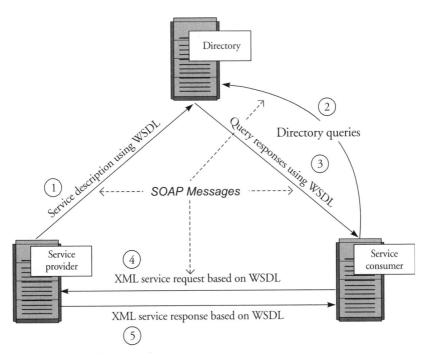

FIGURE 3.3 Web Services basics.

2. A service consumer issues one or more queries to the directory to locate a service and determine how to communicate with that service.

3. Part of the WSDL provided by the service provider is passed to the service consumer. This tells the service consumer what the requests and responses are for the service provider.

4. The service consumer uses the WSDL to send a request to the service provider.

5. The service provider provides the expected response to the service consumer.

Using Universal Description, Discovery, and Integration (UDDI)

The UDDI registry is intended to eventually serve as a means of "discovering" Web Services described using WSDL (see page 205). The idea is that the UDDI registry can be searched in various ways to obtain contact information and the Web Services available for various organizations. Even without the discovery portion, the UDDI registry is a way to keep up-to-date on the Web

Services your organization currently uses. (An alternative to UDDI is the ebXML Registry, which is described on page 208.)

Using SOAP

All the messages shown in Figure 3.3 are sent using SOAP (see page 205). (SOAP at one time stood for Simple Object Access Protocol. Now, the letters in the acronym have no particular meaning.[7]) SOAP essentially provides the envelope for sending the Web Services messages. SOAP generally uses HTTP (see page 225), but other means of connection may be used. HTTP is the familiar connection we all use for the Internet. In fact, it is the pervasiveness of HTTP connections that will help drive the adoption of Web Services.[8]

Figure 3.4 provides more detail on the messages sent using Web Services. At the left of the figure is a fragment of the WSDL sent to the directory. It shows a Customer InfoRequest that requires the customer's account to object information. Also shown is the CustomerInfoResponse that provides a series of items on the customer including name, telephone, and address items.

At the right of Figure 3.4, is a fragment of the WSDL being sent to the service consumer. This is the same fragment sent to the directory by the service provider. The service consumer uses this WSDL to create the service request shown above the arrow connecting the service consumer to the service provider. Upon receiving the request, the service provider returns a message using the format described in the original WSDL. That message appears at the bottom of Figure 3.4.

Using XML with WSDL

WSDL uses XML to define messages. XML has a tagged message format. This is shown in Figure 3.5. The tag `<city>` is highlighted in this figure. The value of city is Burnsville. And `</city>` is the ending tag indicating the end of the value of city. Both the service provider and service consumer use these tags. In fact, the service provider could send the data shown at the bottom of Figure 3.5 in any order. The service consumer uses the tags and not the order of the data to get the data values.

---

7. Starting with SOAP Version 1.2, SOAP is no longer is an acronym.

8. Other protocols are taking advantage of SOAP. For an example, see Blocks Extensible Exchange Protocol (BEEP) on page 205 and ebXML on page 208.

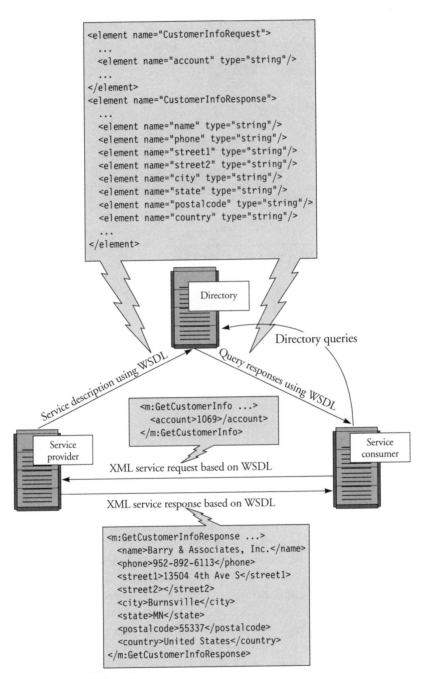

FIGURE 3.4 Web Services messages.

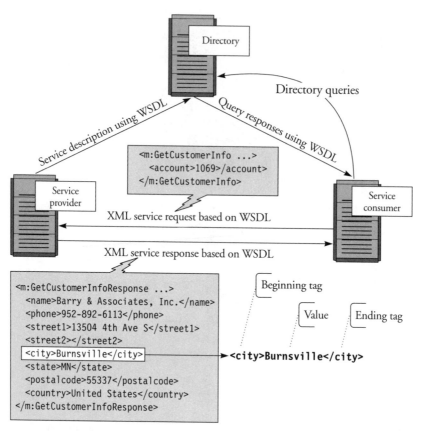

FIGURE 3.5 Tagged messages.

XML Tagged Format Compared to Fixed Record Formats

The XML tagged format provides a level of resilience not available with fixed record formats commonly used before the advent of XML. For example, if a service provider adds an additional element not expected by a service consumer, the XML tagged format allows processing to continue without any problems occurring.

Figure 3.6 shows a service provider adding a new element "extension" for a telephone extension. The service provider sends this to the directory as shown at the left of Figure 3.6. At the bottom of the figure, the service provider is shown providing a response that includes the new element.

Now, it is not uncommon for something to go wrong with our information systems. In this case, what went wrong is that the service consumer did not query the directory to get the new definition. Let's see what happens when XML tagged messages are used.

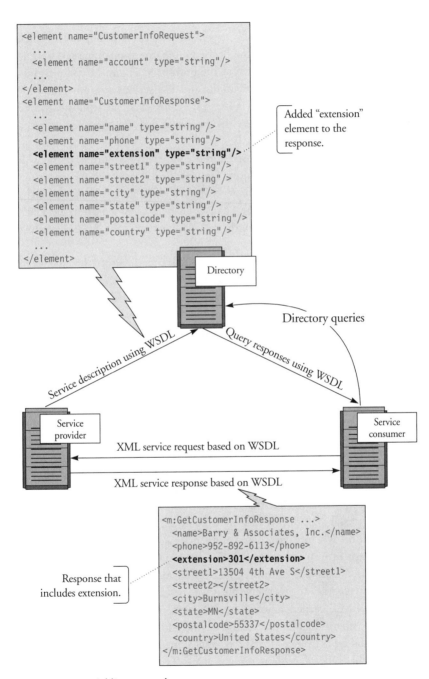

FIGURE 3.6 Adding a new element.

The service consumer does not expect to receive the telephone extension. Nevertheless, because of the XML tagged messages, essentially nothing bad happens when extra data (the value of the phone extension) is passed back by the service provider. This is shown at the bottom of Figure 3.7. The tags are used to identify each of the data items and the service consumer uses the proper values. The extra telephone extension data is simply ignored. Although it might be nice to have the extension data, the good news is that no other data is received incorrectly.

If a fixed record format was used and the same error occurred, there could be harm. Let's look at this situation. Figure 3.8 shows a fixed record format that passes the same information on customers. The length of this record is 124 characters. Now, assume the EXTENSION field is added after the PHONE field, but to keep the record length to 124 characters, the STREET2 field is shortened by three characters.

Figure 3.9 shows this change in the context of a directory. Just as in Figure 3.6, the service provider sends this to the directory as shown at the left of Figure 3.9. Assume the same error occurs as previously described. The service consumer does not query the directory to get the new definition. As a result, the service consumer is unaware that the response is going to contain a value for the telephone extension. Because the fixed record format assumes everything is based on position, whatever appears in a particular position is moved into a field in the service consumer. Figure 3.9 shows that both the EXTENSION and STREET1 fields are moved into the first street address in the service consumer.

Figure 3.10 provides another way to view how this happened. In fixed record messaging, everything is positional. Since the service consumer was unaware of the record change, it moved "30113504 4th Ave S" into the STREET1 field shown at the bottom of Figure 3.10.

The effect of an error like this is interesting. Obviously, if the service consumer sent postal mail to this address, it could not be delivered. Less obvious is the situation when a customer record does not have a phone extension. Then the first three spaces of the STREET1 field in the service consumer would be spaces. If the service consumer sent postal mail to this address, it could then be delivered as long as the address was no longer than 17 characters. If the address line exceeded 17 characters then the last part of the address line would show up on the first part of the second address line. Often, that would mean it could be delivered as well. So, only some addresses would fail. Tracking down this type of error is often not easy. Certainly, more catastrophic errors can occur when changing the structure of fixed length records. There could be situations where the service consumer could even fail because the record layout coming from the service provider is not the layout expected.

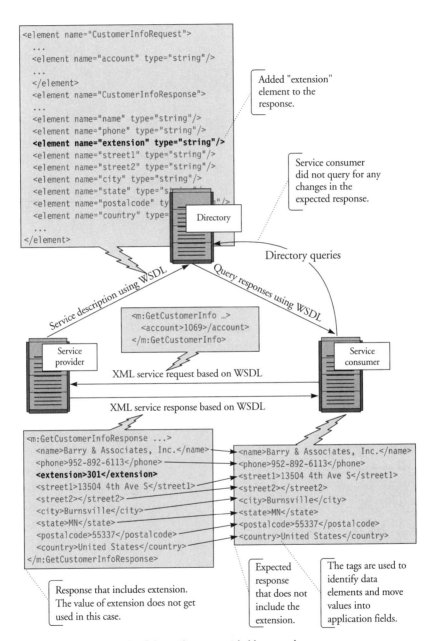

FIGURE 3.7 Example of the resilience provided by tagged messages.

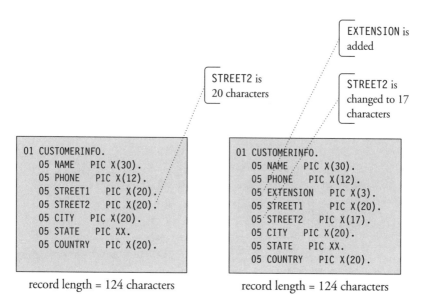

record length = 124 characters   record length = 124 characters

FIGURE 3.8   Record content changes without changing length of record.

These types of errors occur all the time when exchanging data between systems, either internally or between an internal and an external system. Using the XML tagged format makes systems more resilient in the face of these types of error.

The downside of using XML is that the messages are much longer. XML messages are physically longer than fixed record messages because of the included tag information. So, there is a potential performance hit. With XML, you are trading some resilience in your systems for some reduction in performance. Nevertheless, as transmission speeds increase, this reduction in performance may not be noticed.

Options Besides XML

It is possible to have Web Services without XML. If you look at the description of WSDL starting on page 207, you will see the XML is not required. Some organizations might opt for a different message format. One reason to use something other than XML might be the need for extremely high performance. XML-based messages can become large and therefore may not meet some high-performance requirements. If something other than XML is used, both the service provider and the service consumer must agree on the message formats. Within an organization that should be relatively simple. Between

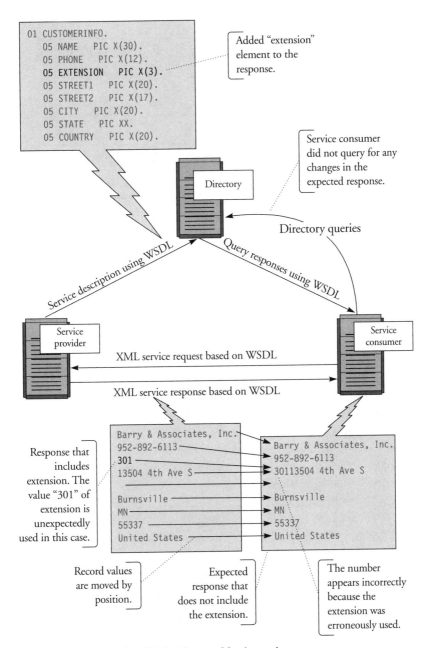

```
01 CUSTOMERINFO.
   05 NAME    PIC X(30).
   05 PHONE   PIC X(12).
   05 EXTENSION    PIC X(3).
   05 STREET1  PIC X(20).
   05 STREET2  PIC X(17).
   05 CITY   PIC X(20).
   05 STATE   PIC XX.
   05 COUNTRY   PIC X(20).
```

Added "extension" element to the response.

Service consumer did not query for any changes in the expected response.

Directory

Directory queries

Service description using WSDL

Query responses using WSDL

Service provider

Service consumer

XML service request based on WSDL

XML service response based on WSDL

```
Barry & Associates, Inc.
952-892-6113
301
13504 4th Ave S

Burnsville
MN
55337
United States
```

```
Barry & Associates, Inc.
952-892-6113
30113504 4th Ave S


Burnsville
MN
55337
United States
```

Response that includes extension. The value "301" of extension is unexpectedly used in this case.

Record values are moved by position.

Expected response that does not include the extension.

The number appears incorrectly because the extension was erroneously used.

FIGURE 3.9 Example of the brittleness of fixed record messages.

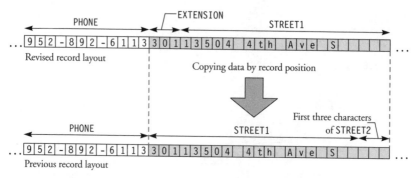

FIGURE 3.10   How the wrong data can be copied using fixed records.

organizations, this can be more difficult. And among all organizations within an industry, this could become intractable. That is why so many industry groups are converging on XML as the way to specify messages. In a sense, it is the least common denominator. Nevertheless, there are economic advantages to having agreement on industry-wide vocabularies for the passing of service messages. A sampling of these vocabularies can be found starting on page 212.

Security and Authorization

At the time this book was written, the hot topic in Web Services was security and authorization. In fact, this is often the reason cited for not proceeding with any work related to Web Services. In the section after the bulleted list, we will see why this is not necessary, but first let's look at security and authorization.

Topics are listed below that relate to security and authorization.[9] These are being worked on in Organization for the Advancement of Structured Information Standards (OASIS) and the World Wide Web Consortium (W3C).[10] (This listing is meant to be reassuring in the breadth of work being done. Unfortunately, as a result, there is quite a bit of jargon in the description. Don't be concerned if the jargon does not mean anything to you at this time.)

- **eXtensible Access Control Markup Language (XACML):** provides fine grained control of authorized activities, the effect of characteristics of the access requestor, the protocol over which the request is made, authorization based on classes of activities, and content introspection.

---

9. Also see the discussion of firewalls starting on page 180.

10. See page 191 for a description of these organizations and other organizations working on standards related to Web Services.

- **eXtensible rights Markup Language (XrML):** a digital rights language designed for securely specifying and managing rights and conditions associated with various resources including digital content as well as services.

- **XML Common Biometric Format (XCBF):** a common set of secure XML encoding for the formats specified in CBEFF, the Common Biometric Exchange File Format.

- **Service Provisioning Markup Language (SPML):** an XML-based framework specification for exchanging user, resource, and service provisioning information. The SPML specification is being developed with consideration of the following provisioning-related specifications: Active Digital Profile (ADPr), eXtensible Resource Provisioning Management (XRPM), and Information Technology Markup Language (ITML).

- **Security Assertion Markup Language (SAML):** an XML framework for exchanging authentication and authorization information.

- **XML Signature:** an XML syntax used for representing signatures on digital content and procedures for computing and verifying such signatures. Signatures provide for data integrity and authentication.

- **XML Encryption:** a process for encrypting/decrypting digital content (including XML documents and portions thereof) and an XML syntax used to represent the encrypted content and information that enables an intended recipient to decrypt it.

- **XML Key Management Specification (XKMS):** a specification of XML application/protocol that allows a simple client to obtain key information (values, certificates, and management or trust data) from a Web service.

It is reasonable to expect these specifications to change shape, merge, and possibly acquire new names and acronyms. You can find the latest information on the status of security and authorization at www.service-architecture.com.

The fact that these specifications are in flux should *not* hold you back from experimenting with Web Services. Much can be done without having the specifications complete. Chapter 7 discusses the stages of adoption for Web Services. The first four of the five stages do not require much security and authorization because they involve internal systems. Of course, how internal systems are used affects the level of security and authorization needed. Nevertheless, nearly all organizations should be able to find some areas to experiment with Web Services that have low requirements for security and authorization.

Simplified Web Services Notation

For the remainder of this book, a simplified notation will be used for Web Services. This is shown in Figure 3.11. In the simplified notation, the directory is implicit in the rectangle labeled "Web Services" at the middle of this figure. You could think of Web Services much like the bus in a PC in which you plug various circuit boards. Other middleware solutions appear similar and use the same "bus" concept, as we will see in the next chapter.

Another important concept in service-oriented architectures is that any service producer could also be a service consumer. This is why Figure 3.11 shows only services at the bottom of the figure under the Web Services bus.

Summary

This chapter outlined service-oriented architectures and Web Services along with ways that organizations of any size can use such architectures. It showed the importance that XML will play in the use of Web Services. XML is the default message format for WSDL. WSDL describes services available through Web Services. The place where the description in WSDL is stored is a directory such as UDDI directory. Directories such as UDDI will function for Web Services much like 411 or telephone directories function for the telephone system. Finally, SOAP is positioned to become the default way to transmit WSDL among services and directories. The chapter ended with a summary of current work on security and authorization related to Web Services along with a caution that it is not necessary to wait for those specifications to be complete before getting started with Web Services.

The use of any technology, of course, must exist in the context of our organizations. Organizations have many forces that affect the adoption of new technology. The next chapter will delve into the forces affecting the adoption Web Services.

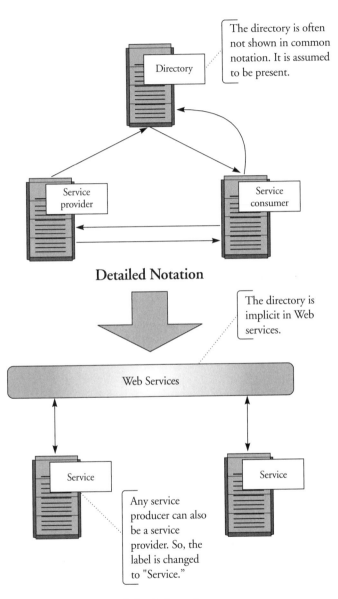

Detailed Notation

The directory is often not shown in common notation. It is assumed to be present.

The directory is implicit in Web services.

Any service producer can also be a service provider. So, the label is changed to "Service."

Simplified Notation

FIGURE 3.11 Simplified Web Services notation.

CHAPTER 4

Forces Affecting the Adoption of Web Services and Other Integration Techniques

Change in any organization can be challenging. This applies to technical and system changes as well. In this chapter, changes in the form of various integration techniques are covered. For each technique, the forces that help and hinder the change are analyzed using a technique called force field analysis. Included in the force field analysis are integration techniques such as adopting enterprise-wide standards, various types of middleware, data warehousing, and message routing.

> ➤ My first exposure to attempting enterprise integration came many years ago. I worked for a corporation that decided to standardize on what was called "basic business elements" or BBEs. Various departments had different definitions for serial numbers, among other commonly used data elements. This was seen as a bad thing that had to be expensive to the corporation. An analogy was made to a discovery that different sheet metal screws were being used to build equipment in different departments when one type of screw could be used almost universally. Buying, inventorying, and using one type of screw actually saved a considerable amount of money. The reasoning, believe it or not, was that if using one type of sheet metal screw across departments saves money, then using one serial number definition across departments should also save money. The intent was good, but of course, a lot of time and money was spent on defining these BBEs. The analysis seemed to go forever. In fact, the use of BBEs never went beyond the analysis stage.

Force Field Analysis Overview

Force field analysis is a tool that can help us get a perspective on the forces at work when trying to make changes in organizations. This approach to analyzing change was developed by Kurt Lewin.[1] Figure 4.1 illustrates the concepts of this technique. For any particular activity, there is a goal or vision, which is shown by the large arrow at the top of the figure pointing to the right. There are driving and restraining forces that will impact whether this goal or vision can be achieved. Driving forces, which help achieve the goal or vision, are shown as arrows pointing to the right in the same direction as the large arrow at the top. Restraining forces, which hinder goal achievement, are the arrows pointing to the left, in the opposite direction as the large arrow at the top. At some point, driving and restraining forces are in equilibrium. This is illustrated in the figure by the wide vertical line labeled "Status Quo." Driving forces move an organization from the status quo in the direction of the organization's goal or vision. Restraining forces hold back this change from the status quo. These forces can be external or internal to an organization, or external or internal to the individuals in the organization. The relative strength of the driving or restraining forces determines whether change occurs.

Assume, for example, that you want to change a part of a system in an organization. An external organizational driving force could be the opportu-

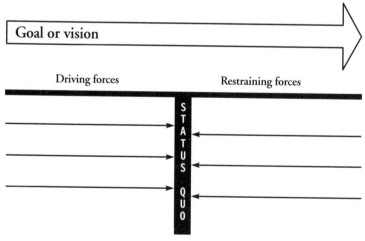

FIGURE 4.1 Force field analysis.

---

1. Lewin, Kurt, *Field Theory in Social Science,* Harper and Row, New York, 1951.

nity to electronically exchange purchase orders and invoices with a particular customer or supplier. An internal organizational driving force could be a reduction in operating costs. An internal organizational restraining force could be the development cost for making the change. Finally, an internal individual restraining force for some people in the company might be that the change to the system may result in fewer jobs in their part of the organization. Figure 4.2 illustrates this concept.

Of course, there could be many other forces at work than those shown in Figure 4.2. The nature of the driving and restraining forces could also vary by organization even if the organizations were attempting to carry out exactly the same tasks. In fact, they can vary among departments in the same organization.

Essentially, the purpose of this model is to make all the driving and restraining forces visible so that decisions concerning change can be made with the best available information. There are various ways to use this model. If you want to make change more likely, you need to either strengthen the driving forces or weaken the restraining forces. Weakening the restraining forces is sometimes the best approach. Strengthening the driving forces can make the restraining forces get stronger. In Figure 4.2, promoting the electronic interchange capabilities of this change will likely cause more concern about job loss that, in turn, could create various forms of resistance that can effectively scuttle efforts to change from the status quo. So, perhaps it is possible to assure people that jobs will not be lost, thus weakening this restraining force. Of course, this assurance and the resulting reduction in resistance

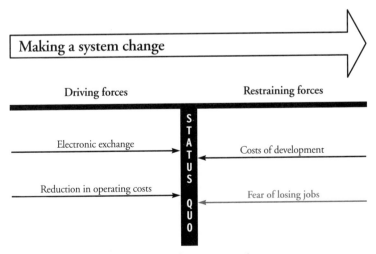

FIGURE 4.2 Force field analysis for making a system change.

would work only if it were actually true that jobs would not be lost. In the figures that follow, weakened restraining forces will be shown as gray arrows to indicate the restraining force is fading away. Figure 4.2, for example, shows that the fear of losing jobs is weakened and less of a concern.

Analysis of Integration Techniques

Common system integration techniques are presented approximately in chronological order. Chronological order allows us to see how, over time, advances in technology and standards have diminished the number of restraining forces, making change more likely to occur. At the end, Web Services will be seen as having the least number of restraining forces compared to any of the other techniques. Using Web Services essentially represents the most recent advance in standards and technology.

The force field analysis presented here will highlight common driving and restraining forces. Every organization will, of course, have additional forces to consider that might be unique to the organization. Also, design issues such as "project scope" or people issues such as "resistance to change" do not appear in these analyses, because they will require special discussion. These issues will be covered in Part II of this book on managing change.

Also, each analysis will include such driving forces as "reduced development time" and "reduced maintenance cost" as universal driving forces.

Analysis of Adopting Enterprise-Wide Standards

The most obvious way to integrate systems within any organization is to establish some type of enterprise-wide standards. This section will cover the forces affecting the adoption of standard data element definitions and the adoption of standard, enterprise software.

Adopting Standard Data Element Definitions

This first analysis shown in Figure 4.3 relates to the vignette that opened this chapter. In the early 1980s, many large organizations were running on custom software and there was very little use of packaged software. At the time, it was believed that there would be opportunities to exchange data more easily, reduce development time, and possibly reduce maintenance costs if all the custom software were to use the same data element definitions. These opportunities are shown as driving forces in Figure 4.3. Restraining forces related to cost offset these driving forces of saving money. Figure 4.3 shows the restrain-

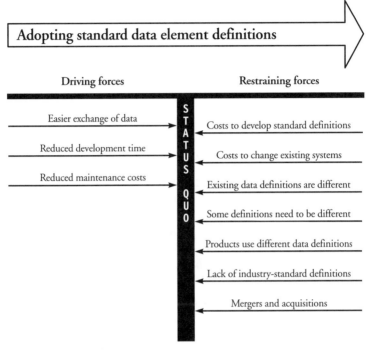

FIGURE 4.3 Force field analysis for adopting standard data element definitions.

ing forces of costs to developing the standard definitions and the costs related to changing the existing systems.

There are additional restraining forces in this figure. In some cases, there were valid reasons that two different systems used different definitions for the same data element. For example, in the vignette opening this chapter, most of the differences related to serial numbers and how they were used among different departments. Also, in the early 1980s, there had been little progress in developing a standard set of data elements for industry. Therefore, the cost of developing a standard set for an organization was quite high because it involved starting with a clean sheet of paper. Even if this effort to change to standard data elements had been successful, the first merger or acquisition would likely cause a problem. The systems used by every other organization would have used different data elements. Finally, as the use of packaged software increased, the definitions used in those products would most likely be incompatible. With enough mergers or acquisitions and use of packaged software, you would be back at the starting point with incompatibility of data definitions.

➤ *Times have changed since the early 1980s and so have attitudes toward standard data elements. Some industries can see advantages in having standard data elements so that data can easily be interchanged. Another advantage to standard data elements is that they lessen the integration efforts involved in mergers and acquisitions. A sampling of standard vocabularies by industry starts on page 212. So, it would be fair to say that the infrastructure provided by Web Services and XML has given a boost to the standardization efforts.*

Adopting Standard, Enterprise-Wide Software

In some organizations, there is great interest in establishing organization-wide software. This works sometimes. When it does, however, usually it is successful only for a short period. The appeal of adopting standard software is obviously that everyone uses the same software. This means that the entire organization uses the same data definitions, semantics, and formats for exchanging data. Usually this works best for organizations that are small and putting a new set of systems in place. It also works if you are standardizing on non-systems software such as a particular word processor, spreadsheet, or an e-mail system. Nevertheless, standardizing on systems software often runs into problems, too. There are long-term restraining forces, such as mergers and acquisitions that can come into play. Even a new, small organization can acquire another company that uses an entirely different system, and integration problems begin. Figure 4.4 provides the force field analysis for standard, enterprise-wide software.

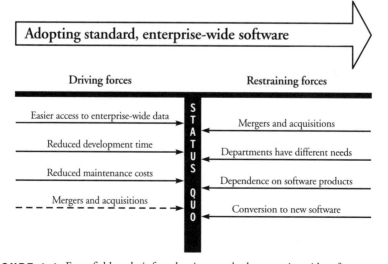

FIGURE 4.4 Force field analysis for adopting standard, enterprise-wide software.

Beside the mergers and acquisitions restraining force, it is common in larger organizations that some departments have different software needs. It is rare that you can find "one size fits all" software. Another downside is that adopting a complete set of software systems from a single vendor makes your organization dependent on that single vendor. As soon as you move away from that vendor's products, you might be back into common integration issues. Finally, for organizations that have existing systems, adopting standard software can mean a mass conversion to the new software. This often is problematic and should be seen as a restraining force.

Note that none of the restraining forces in this figure are shown in gray. This means that they will not diminish over time and will remain restraining forces going forward into the foreseeable future.

There is, however, increasing recognition among software vendors that it is in their interest to create plug-compatible software components that can be used in assembling a service-oriented architecture. This plug-compatibility will be achieved using Web Services. Using plug-compatible software will make it easier to "mix and match" vendor products when developing or modifying an enterprise architecture.

Of course, every example has a counter example. There are some industries where mergers and acquisitions are commonplace. You will see organizations in those industries adopting common, industry-wide software packages so that it will be easier for one organization to be acquired or merged with another organization. So, mergers and acquisitions can also be a driving force. This is represented in Figure 4.4 with a dashed line. Although, I have not seen any empirical data on this, my experience is that this is the exception rather than the rule. That is the reason for the dashed line because it is likely to not apply to all industries. Similarly, mergers and acquisitions could be a driving force for current efforts on developing industry-wide vocabularies for Web Services.[2]

Analysis of Middleware Integration

Middleware hides the complexity of the communication between two or more systems or services. This simplifies the development of those systems and services and isolates the complexity of the communication between them. The different systems or services can be on the same hardware or on different hardware. Figure 4.5 shows the basic middleware architecture.

---

2. See page 212 for a sampling of industry-wide vocabularies.

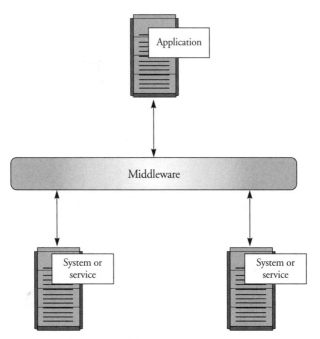

FIGURE 4.5 Basic middleware architecture.

In Figure 4.5, the different systems and services each are running on different machines. These machines could be in the same location or different locations for the same organization. Alternatively, all three machines could belong to different organizations.

There has been significant work on middleware over the years. Some examples of middleware include:

- **Transaction processing (TP) monitors.** A TP monitor ensures that transactions process completely or the appropriate action is taken if an error occurs. They often employ load balancing because a transaction may be forwarded to any of several servers.

- **Remote Procedure Call (RPC).** An RPC allows execution of program logic on a remote system by calling a local routine.

- **Message-Oriented Middleware (MOM).** MOM provides program-to-program data exchange.

- **Object Request Broker (ORB)**. An ORB allows a system to request a service without knowing anything about what servers are available. The request is forwarded to the appropriate services with the results of the request returned to the requesting system.

This section will examine adopting two forms of existing middleware and compare that to adopting Web Services as middleware. The two forms commonly used are the Object Management Group's Common Object Request Broker Architecture (CORBA) specification and Microsoft's Distributed Common Object Model (DCOM).

Adopting CORBA and DCOM

CORBA and DCOM are middleware that provide a means for applications to communicate with each other. CORBA is a set of specifications developed through the Object Management Group (see page 222). Implementations of CORBA are referred to as *ORBs* or *object request brokers.* DCOM comes from Microsoft (see page 223). CORBA and DCOM are interoperable through CORBA/DCOM bridges. Both CORBA and DCOM represent reasonably mature technology for creating interoperable, networked applications. Figure 4.6 shows that providing interoperable, networked applications are a driving force for adopting CORBA, DCOM, or in some cases both.

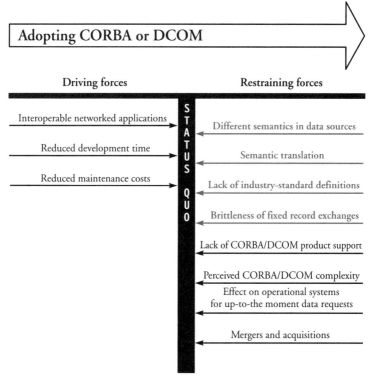

FIGURE 4.6 Force field analysis for adopting CORBA or DCOM.

CORBA and DCOM, however, are the means to get data from one place to another. There are no specific requirements for the format of the data transmitted in the messages, which means that the transmitted data might not be workable when it arrives at its destination. The restraining forces related to data exist with either CORBA or DCOM. These are:

- Different semantics in data sources

- Semantic translation

- Lack of industry-standard definitions

Advances in industry standards for XML,[3] EDI,[4] and Web Services (see page 205) will mitigate all these restraining forces, which is why they are shown as gray arrows in Figure 4.6. In fact, using XML (see page 209) with CORBA or DCOM makes for a more flexible system because of the tagged record structure of XML.[5] This would also mitigate the restraining force related to the brittleness of fixed record formats.

There is a perception in the industry that neither CORBA nor DCOM are that widely adopted and that using one or the other—or both—is too complex for many programmers. Whether the perceived lack of industry adoption or inherent complexity is actually true is irrelevant at this point. These perceptions are seen as restraining forces. In fact, they should be seen as the most significant restraining forces. Web Services have just the opposite perception—they are seen as easy to adopt widely by industry and easy for most programmers to use. Perception in this case might well be the reality.

The very nature of creating interoperable, networked resources means that there could be a negative impact on operational systems when requests come in through CORBA or DCOM. Many operational systems have not been designed to receive ad hoc or unexpected processing requests. These requests sometimes can have a negative impact on the performance of those systems. So, the effect on operations systems can be a restraining force, but should be expected if up-to-the-moment processing is needed (see page 161).

Finally, mergers and acquisitions could be an issue because it is entirely possible that the acquired systems do not use either CORBA or DCOM, and it is not a trivial task to retrofit systems to use either technology.

---

3. A sample of industry-specific XML vocabularies are listed starting on page 212.

4. The ebXML Registry is an example for EDI. It is discussed on page 208.

5. For an explanation of the tagged record structure of XML and the brittleness of fixed record formats, see page 26.

Adopting Web Services

Using Web Services is the missing piece in the puzzle of how to create interoperable systems and services and benefits from the development of CORBA and DCOM. Web Services use of both XML and HTTP[6] on the Internet greatly reduces restraining forces that existed with preceding technologies. The perceived simplicity of Web Services has created a stampede of vendors incorporating Web Services into their products and services. Figure 4.7 shows the driving and restraining forces for adopting Web Services.

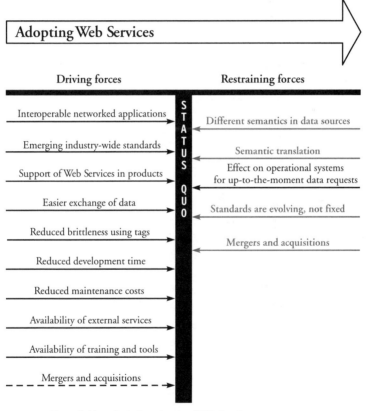

FIGURE 4.7 Force field analysis for adopting Web Services.

---

6. One reason other protocols have failed to gain wide acceptance is the desire to use HTTP. The CORBA Internet Inter-ORB Protocol (IIOP) is an example of a protocol that did not gain wide acceptance, in part for that reason.

In addition to the same driving force of interoperable, networked applications shown for CORBA and DCOM, the driving forces in Figure 4.7 now include a driving force related to XML's tagged format: reduced brittleness using tags. The explosive growth of Web Services being used in products will also result in a significant growth of external services that can be used by organizations of any size. The nature of services available will be covered in Chapter 5. Similarly, there is an abundance of training and tools becoming available on Web Services.

The restraining forces are similar to those we have seen with earlier integration techniques. These include:

• Different semantics in data sources

• Semantic translation

There is a tremendous amount of work in various standards organizations to simplify the semantics and standardize the semantic translation (see page 212). Those standards are evolving, which is why it is seen as a restraining force. Nevertheless, as time goes on, these restraining forces will weaken.

Finally, mergers and acquisitions, which appeared as a restraining force for CORBA and DCOM, is shown in Figure 4.7 as a weakening restraining force for the adoption of Web service. The broad adoption of Web Services by product vendors over time increases the likelihood that an acquired company will be able to work with Web Services. Mergers and acquisitions also appear as a driving force. This is for those industries where mergers and acquisitions are commonplace. Mergers and acquisitions could, for example, be a driving force for current efforts on developing industry-wide vocabularies for Web Services (see page 212). The reason for the dashed line in Figure 4.7 is because this driving force is likely to not apply to all industries.

Just as with CORBA and DCOM, you are left with the possible impact on operational systems, but this should be expected if up-to-the-moment processing is needed. As mentioned in that discussion many operational systems have not been designed to receive ad hoc or unexpected processing requests. These requests sometimes can have a negative impact on the performance of those systems. So, the effect on operations systems can be a restraining force, but should be expected if up-to-the-moment processing is needed.

Adopting Web Services Does Not Mean Abandoning CORBA or DCOM

For organizations that have invested heavily in CORBA or DCOM, the adoption of Web Services does not mean you need to abandon CORBA or DCOM and convert existing systems. Recall that the middleware hides the complexity of the communication between two more systems or services. That hiding of complexity allows existing systems to participate in Web Services by altering the way the middleware works. Figure 4.8 is a high-level view of how Web Services can work with both CORBA and DCOM with each of the systems or services operating in a different organization.[7]

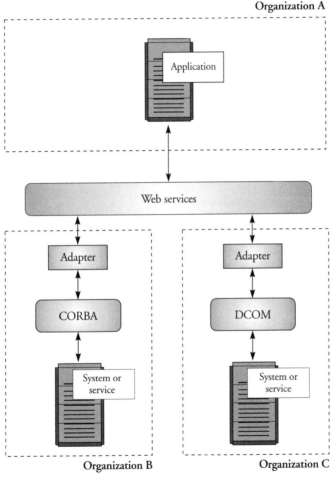

FIGURE 4.8 Web Services interoperating with CORBA and DCOM.

---

7. Of course, a similar figure could be drawn for other forms of middleware. Web Services is helping to drive the interoperability of all forms of middleware.

Analysis of Additional Components Used for Integration in a Service-Oriented Architecture

Two additional techniques of integration can be used in a service-oriented architecture. They are data warehousing and message routing. This section discusses those techniques and how they can be integrated with middleware such as CORBA, DCOM, and Web Services. Also, this section will show how efforts around Web Services will enhance both data warehousing and message routing.

Analysis of Data Warehousing

One of the oldest and most successful ways to integrate data from multiple systems is to extract that data from existing systems and load it into a single, central location to form an enterprise data warehouse (EDW). Using an EDW can be complementary to using CORBA, DCOM, or Web Services. The analysis for this approach is shown in Figure 4.9.

In this figure, the easier exchange of data as a driving force is replaced with easier access to enterprise-wide data. This data is loaded from existing systems using various techniques that extract, transform, and load the data in the EDW. Using extract, transform, and load (ETL) techniques means there is usually less impact on operational systems because the extracts of data from these systems could be done at a time convenient for the operational system. This lowered impact on operational systems is a significant driving force. Easier access to enterprise-wide data also allows the use of business intelligence (BI) software to find patterns or new business opportunities based on a wealth of data that could be stored in an EDW (see page 220).

Most of the restraining forces are issues with the semantics or meaning of the data and the standardization of data definitions. Not surprisingly, these issues are similar to those involved with attempts at adopting standard data elements when existing data definitions are different. In this figure, the semantic translation is added to show the need to transform data can itself be a restraining force. Over time, however, these restraining forces have become weaker for two reasons:

1. **A subset of our industry is devoted to the development of ETL software.** This software generally simplifies the development the data extractions from existing systems, any semantic translation or transformation, and the loading of the data into the EDW.

2. **More industry standards have become available.** Initially with efforts related to Electronic Data Interchange (EDI) and more recently with Web Services.

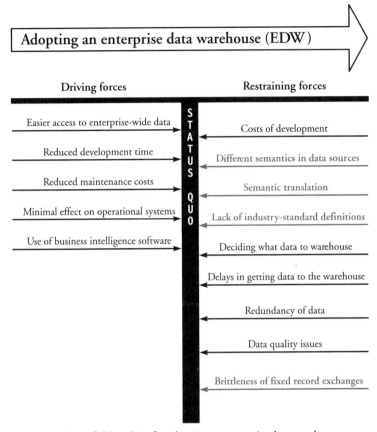

FIGURE 4.9 Force field analysis for adopting an enterprise data warehouse.

Additional restraining forces include problems related to what data to store in the EDW, and the delay or latency of getting data into the EDW. The issue of what data should be stored in an EDW will likely always remain a restraining force. The strength of this restraining force will vary by organization. The delay or latency of data is the result of performing data extracts at times convenient to the operational systems.[8] Consequently, the very latest data is not always available in the EDW. To some organizations, this is no problem. Others, however, may find this a significant restraining force.

Redundancy of data also can be seen as a restraining force. Whenever data exists in more than one location, it is possible that the data will have different

---

8. For some organizations, this can be a certain time of day. For others who cannot stop their operational systems, it may be necessary to provide small data extracts throughout the day.

values for various reasons. This could result, in part, from the latency of data mentioned earlier. For example, the value of an account balance may be updated by the operational system but not forwarded to the EDW until some later date. At a given point in time, you could see two different values for the same account when looking at the EDW and the operational system. Often, the way to resolve redundancy issues is to create a master database that all systems should use.

Data quality issues are potentially a restraining force, because much depends on the quality of the data available. If data to be stored in the EDW is lacking in quality, there are options available for improving its quality. Changes could be made to improve data quality at the time it is entered. For existing data, the quality could be improved at the source. If that is not possible, the ETL software used to load data could be used to improve the quality of the data. Sometimes this is called *data cleansing* (see page 222). This, of course, assumes the quality can be improved in some way that lends itself to programming. Data quality is a significant topic and you are encouraged to study it further if this is potentially a restraining force for your organization.

Finally, the brittleness of fixed record exchanges is a maintenance issue (see page 26). If the EDW is changed in some way, it could create a need to change some or all the ETL programs. Because of the nature of fixed record exchanges, there is always a chance that not all ETL programs were updated and the wrong data is extracted. As a result, the transform and load portion could fail or the wrong portion of the record could be inappropriately transformed and loaded into the EDW resulting in essentially a corrupted EDW. This brittleness problem is being addressed by the tagged record structure of XML (see page 26). The tagged structure significantly reduces that chance of corrupting the data in the EDW and also presents the opportunity to reduce maintenance costs related to ETL programs (see page 224). So, as a restraining force, the brittleness of fixed records will be reduced. Many of the restraining forces will be reduced because of efforts related to industry standards, XML, and Web Services as represented by the gray arrows in Figure 4.9.

Use of an EDW can be coupled with the use of CORBA, DCOM, or Web Services as shown in Figure 4.10.

Analysis of Application or Message Routing

Often when integrating systems, there is also a need to propagate data among internal systems. For example, it is believable that if a customer's address were changed in one internal system, you would want that change to appear as soon as possible in other internal systems.

If each internal system were directly connected to the other internal systems shown at the bottom of Figure 2.1, you could have up to 15 intercon-

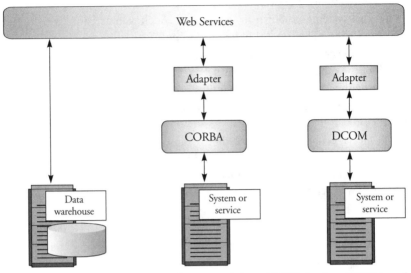

FIGURE 4.10 Enterprise data warehouse co-existing with Web Services, CORBA, and DCOM.

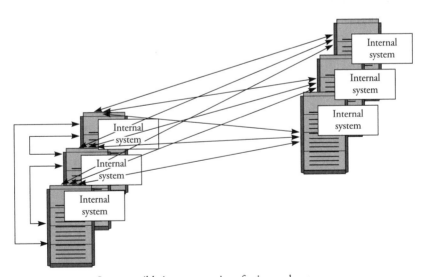

FIGURE 4.11 Some possible interconnections for internal systems.

nections. Some of those connections are shown in Figure 4.11. Of course, if you need to propagate an update, such as a customer address, to multiple systems, you could end up in the situation shown in Figure 4.11. In this situation, every system potentially may need to communicate to other internal systems.

Architecturally, a good solution to this problem is to add a *message router* to internal systems as shown in Figure 4.12. Such routers have been around for some time. They are also known as *application routers.* This message router, however, would be based on Web Services. Also, a router could know which of the other internal systems needs to receive a certain type of updates. The individual internal systems would not need to know who receives such updates. As a result, the number of interconnections is reduced as shown in Figure 4.12.

A message router usually needs to transform the data in some way to match the format of the data expected by the receiving system. Figure 4.13 shows examples of such transformations. Internal system A at the left is sending data in tagged XML format. Internal system B at the right expects a tagged XML format, but expects the tags to be different. For example, instead of the tag <name> in system A, system B expects the data to be tagged with <customer>. The tags for phone and postal code data also are different. The message tag itself varies as well. At the left, the tag is <GetCustomerInfo-Response> and at the right, the tag is <GetCustomerAccount>. Finally, System C expects a fixed record format. This fixed format is shown at the bottom of Figure 4.13. The message router needs to "know" how to make these transformations.

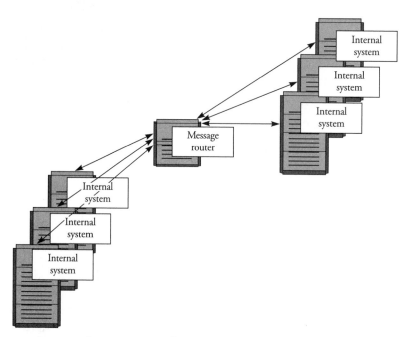

FIGURE 4.12 Interconnections when using a message router.

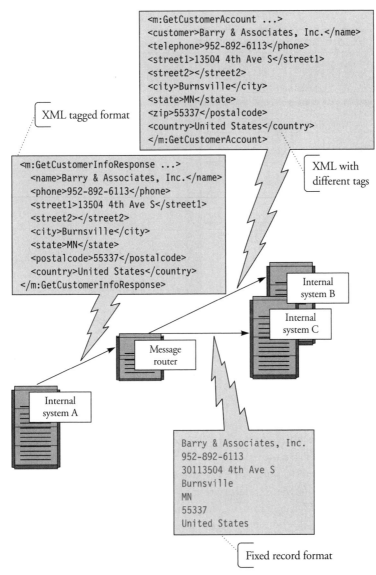

FIGURE 4.13 Transformations in a message router.

In some ways, a message router is the flip side of EDW. Message routing disperses data where EDW collects data. Nevertheless, the analyses of the two approaches are similar. The analysis for adopting a message router is shown in Figure 4.14. In this figure, a driving force is consistent enterprise-wide data in all applications. This means that customer data, for example, would be the

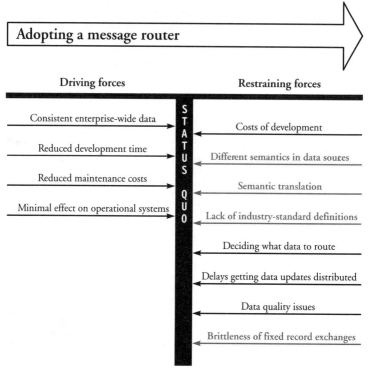

FIGURE 4.14 Force field analysis for adopting a message router.

same no matter what system used or managed that data. The impact on operational systems is also lowered since any one system only needs to communicate with the message router and not all the other internal systems.

Most of the restraining forces are the issues with the semantics or meaning of the data and the standardization of data definitions that have been discussed earlier. Message routing, like EDW, needs to deal with semantic translation and this is shown as a restraining force. Over time, however, these restraining forces have become weaker as more industry standards become available.

Additional restraining forces include problems related to what data to route and the delay or latency of getting data updates distributed to various internal systems. The issues of what data to route and the delay of getting data updates distributed will likely always remain a restraining force.

Data quality issues similar to EDW can occur with message routing. Obviously, it can be potentially disastrous to route poor quality data. With message routing, however, you do not have the option of data cleansing used in conjunction with ETL software. The quality of data needs to be improved at the source for existing data and at the point of entry for new data.

Finally, the brittleness of fixed record exchanges is a maintenance issue.[9] If the format of the record going to the message router is changed in some way, it could create a problem. Because of the nature of fixed record exchanges, there is always a chance that the wrong data is routed. This brittleness problem is being addressed by the tagged record structure of XML. The tagged structure significantly reduces that chance of corrupting the data in the message router and presents the opportunity to reduce maintenance costs related to message routing programs. So, as a restraining force, the brittleness of fixed records will be reduced over time.

Web Services adapters for packaged software provided by vendors will also reduce costs of development. The adapters allow Web Services connections with internally developed systems or packaged software. The arrow depicting that restraining force of development cost, however, is not shown as gray since there are still other significant development costs related to a message router. Nevertheless, many of the restraining forces will be reduced because of efforts related to industry standards, XML, and Web Services as represented by the gray arrows in Figure 4.14.

When a message router uses Web Services, it is depicted in this book as shown in Figure 4.15. Essentially, all the same data paths shown in Figures 4.11 and 4.12 are retained. For the purposes of creating a readable figure, only one line is shown connecting to the message router. This figure also shows two of the internal systems using an adapter. This is meant to represent that some internal systems may need adapters that are not part of the internal system. These adapters could be written in-house or purchased from third-party software vendors.

Just like EDW, message routing can also work with existing middleware solutions such as CORBA and DCOM. This is shown in Figure 4.16. The message router would have connections to Web Services that, in turn, would connect to CORBA and DCOM. As explained earlier, the message router would "know" what data should be routed and when, in some cases, the identifying tag might need to be changed for the receiver of the data.

Putting All the Integration Techniques Together in a Service-Oriented Architecture

Middleware integration, data warehousing, and message routing all work together in a service-oriented architecture. Figure 4.17 shows all these technologies as components of a service-oriented architecture. This is essentially a

---

9. For an explanation of the brittleness of fixed formats, see page 26.

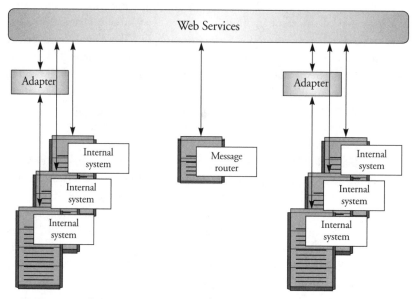

FIGURE 4.15 A message router using Web Services.

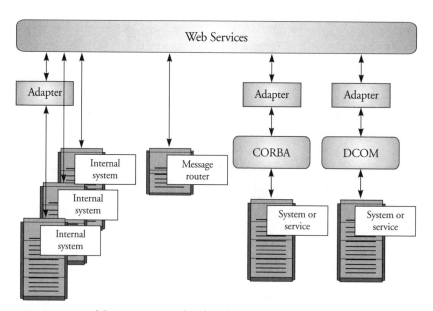

FIGURE 4.16 Message router used with Web Services, CORBA, and DCOM.

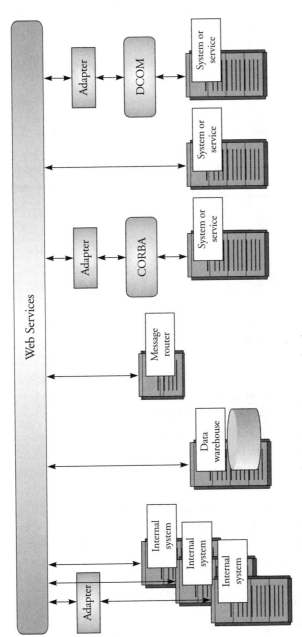

FIGURE 4.17 Multiple components of a service-oriented architecture.

more detailed diagram of C. R.'s organization, which was described in Chapter 2. In Figure 2.1 at the bottom, you can see the internal systems in C. R.'s organization along with the online repository. The three internal systems at the left in Figure 2.1 relate to the three systems at the left in Figure 4.17; this time we add the detail of an adapter for one of the internal systems. The three internal systems at the right in Figure 2.1 relate to the three systems at the right in Figure 4.17; this time one system is CORBA based, a second uses Web Services directly, and a third is DCOM-based. The online repository at the bottom, middle in Figure 2.1 is shown as a message router and a data warehouse in Figure 4.17. Finally, Figure 4.17 shows that C. R.'s organization uses Web Services as the means of interconnecting systems. This detail is not shown in Figure 2.1.

Summary

This chapter used force field analysis to show how various forces drive or restrain the adoption of integration techniques. The discussion showed that using Web Services reduces barriers to integration:

- There are far fewer restraining forces for adopting Web Services than for adopting enterprise-wide standard data element definitions or enterprise-wide software.

- Within middleware, the restraining forces for adopting CORBA or DCOM are much stronger than restraining forces for adopting Web Services. Also, adopting Web Services has more driving forces.

- The standardization efforts related to the use of XML by Web Services are assisting other integration techniques. This was shown in the weakening restraining forces for adopting an enterprise data warehouse and/or a message router.

- Because the use of Web Services does not require abandoning CORBA or DCOM, there are no required changes to existing CORBA or DCOM-based systems. This further reduces barriers to the adoption of Web Services as part of an integration strategy.

The next chapter will cover how the impact of Web Services will grow over time. It uses one of the most significant integration efforts of all time, Electronic Data Interchange, to illustrate the growing impact of Web Services.

CHAPTER 5

Growing Impact of Web Services

Using Web Services has the potential to impact software and systems at all levels. On a simple level, you can use Web Services to create a Web site feature or to create custom portals. On a more complex level, Web Services can serve as the basis for very sophisticated business-to-business software. As time goes on, it is entirely possible that the use of Web Services will introduce revolutionary ways of using the Internet for commercial and personal uses. This chapter provides examples of the initial impact of Web Services in improving Web site and internal system connections. It then uses the example of Electronic Data Interchange (EDI) to show the possibilities that the growing impact of Web Services can have on business-to-business connections.

➤ A distinguishing characteristic of service-oriented architectures is their emphasis on the connections between services using Web Services. These connections will eventually evolve into plug-compatible services upon which we will build our information technology systems. The assembly will be more like making the desired connections among AV components in a home entertainment system than mapping out an enterprise architecture. Like AV components, services could be assembled in multiple ways depending on what we want to get out of our system. And with a service-oriented architecture, you just know that something is going to be invented that either you always wished you had or something that you couldn't have imagined. This might be the equivalent of a digital video recorder or a music file-sharing program. When it happens, you want to have an approach that lets you take advantage of these new ideas and technologies that will come with a service-oriented architecture using Web Services.

Initial Impact of Web Services

Initially, the impact of Web Services on software and systems will be incremental. Web Services will be used to enhance existing software and systems. This is because Web Services are about creating connections. So, Web Services will be used to improve the connections that a Web site uses, connections internal to organizations, or the connections used by business-to-business software.

Improving Web Site Connections

Early examples of Web Services include such things as *gadgets* that can be added to a Web site or portal. Gadgets include such things as customizable stock quotes, weather reports, and news feeds. Such gadgets have been available using other technology, but Web Services essentially makes these gadgets better because they are more customizable. In fact, you can create your own sophisticated Web site for such things as selling books when, in reality, the actual bookstore is located on a different Web site. The content, shopping cart, and other bookstore features come from the real bookstore Web site; the Web Services available from the bookstore Web site allow you customize your Web site to appear as if it is an actual bookstore Web site. Using gadgets in this way is illustrated in Figure 5.1. In this figure, each of the items that appear on the screen from the Web site came from a different Web site. Yet, the viewer is likely to be unaware of how these services are assembled on the Web site. Yes, it blurs where content comes from. But it also opens the opportunity for highly useful Web sites with sophisticated content from multiple sources.

Portals can expand on this type of incremental connectivity by using Web Services adapters (see page 219) to existing systems. For example, a medical records portal could include a patient's medical history, scanned versions of paper documents, X-rays, and laboratory test results. This is illustrated in Figure 5.2. The adapters allow Web Services connections with internally developed systems or packaged software. In this figure, all the systems belong to the same organization and were developed before Web Services became available. This is why each system uses an adapter. Such adapters may not be necessary as systems are developed with Web Services in mind. In addition to using internal systems for a portal, it would also be possible to combine information from the Internet. Perhaps for some patients, information on pollen count from a weather site on the Internet could be combined with the medical records information on a customized portal.

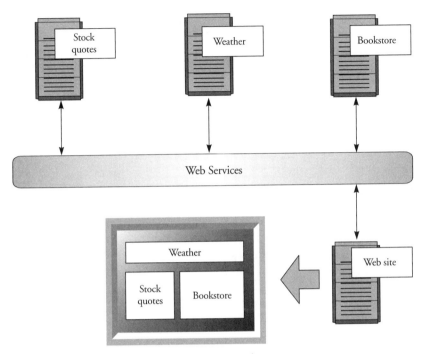

FIGURE 5.1 Using external Web Services in a Web site.

Improving Internal Connections

Since nearly the beginning of the computer industry, developers have sought ways to share data among programs and systems. Early examples involved the sharing of punch cards and tapes. Now, we have generally progressed to more advanced ways to connect internal systems. Internal connections are often made using CORBA, DCOM, proprietary vendor solutions, or internally developed solutions. Web Services initially will be used to improve and standardize those internal connections.

Using Web Services provides a standard connection between systems. The computer industry has virtually stampeded to incorporate Web Services into existing products and to create new products that make it easier to connect systems. This broad adoption makes Web Services the easiest standard to follow for connecting systems going forward.

The use of Web Services can also improve the resilience of your internal connections. It is most likely that your current internal connections use some form of a fixed record layout for the messages sent between systems. The

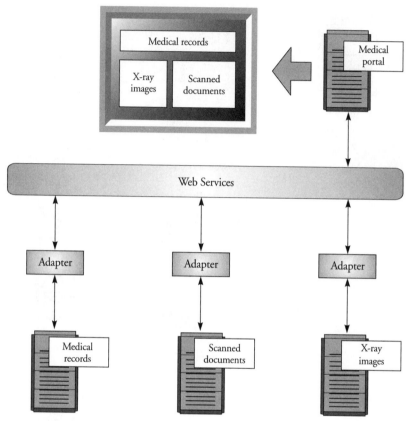

FIGURE 5.2 Using Web Services in medical portal.

errors that can occur because of fixed record layouts was described in Chapter 3, starting on page 26. That description also showed how XML provides greater resilience in the face of simple programming errors.

But you do not need to switch everything to Web Services all at once. Web Services can be adopted incrementally and used in conjunction with current means of connecting internal systems. In the last chapter, starting on page 43, the use of middleware as an integration technique was discussed. Figure 4.8 at the end of that chapter showed how Web Services could be used in conjunction with both CORBA and DCOM. This could apply to other proprietary vendor solutions and internally developed connections as well.

Improving Business-to-Business Connections

Web Services will enhance the existing specifications for business-to-business communication. For many larger organizations, this communication has been based on EDI specification. EDI is a good way to show how Web Services will enhance business-to-business connections.

Many of the issues related to EDI are similar to making any type of connection for the communication of data between systems or services. For this reason, the historical development of EDI will be covered in some detail. This will show how, eventually, Web Services will simplify making connections and make it easier to create a service-oriented architecture.

EDI has been around a long time. Depending on how you determine its start, EDI began as early as the late 1960s. There have been significant efforts on standards for EDI. Two standards efforts are in the INCITS (ANSI) ASC X12 committee and United Nations/Electronic Data Interchange For Administration, Commerce, and Transport (UN/EDIFACT). There are additional standards efforts conducted by other organizations, often to meet the needs of specific industries. Web Services can enhance these standards efforts by making EDI easier for organizations to adopt.

To date, primarily large organizations have adopted EDI. Smaller organizations have felt little impact by EDI. Even among the larger organizations, EDI is often used for simple transactions such as orders, invoices, and delivery notices. There is much greater potential for EDI, as we will see later in this chapter.

A Brief History of EDI

There have been many barriers to the adoption of EDI. Web Services will reduce those barriers, allowing EDI to be used by more organizations and eventually in ways that are more extensive. A good way to understand the barriers is to look at the history of EDI. As we move through the history, the barriers will be discussed and towards the end of this discussion, we will see why Web Services will allow EDI to be used by more organizations.

Figure 5.3 shows the initial form of EDI data transmission. Using EDI involved the following steps:

1. Creating an export file from the sending system.

2. Running the export file through EDI translation software to create a transmission file. The EDI translation software might have been purchased software or software developed in-house.

3. Sending the transmission file to the receiving organization. The transmission file uses a fixed record format since that was the standard at the time. The network at the time was most likely a proprietary network.

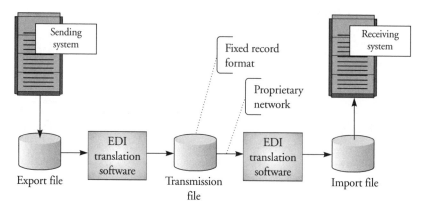

FIGURE 5.3 Initial form of EDI data transmission.

4. Running the transmission file through different EDI translation software in the receiving organization to create an import file compatible with the receiving system.

If a sending organization was participating with multiple receiving organizations, all aspects of the transmission process had to be worked out for every receiving organization. More organizations resulted in more complexity to keep the details of all connections synchronized.

Relatively quickly, the need was seen to improve on this form of EDI data transmission. Value-Added Networks (VANs) were developed to simplify complexity of multiple data connections. Figure 5.4 illustrates EDI using VANs.

VANs provide functions such as message transmission, tracking, and in most cases, security. Using a VAN means that an organization needs to only deal with the VAN instead of connecting to every receiving organization. As such, the VAN acts as a broker, which simplifies using EDI for both sending and receiving organizations. As Figure 5.4 shows, the VANs usually used a proprietary network and continued to use fixed record formats since that was still the standard. EDI translation software continued to be needed at both the sending and receiving organizations.

One major barrier to widespread use of VANs was the cost. EDI with VANs could cost in the vicinity of $100,000 or more per year. This was probably the main reason smaller organizations did not participate in EDI.

CORBA and DCOM entered into use with EDI in an effort to reduce the cost of EDI and to further standardize message transmission. Both CORBA and DCOM provide the basic brokering capabilities provided by VANs. In some case, the VANs adopted either CORBA or DCOM. At first, however,

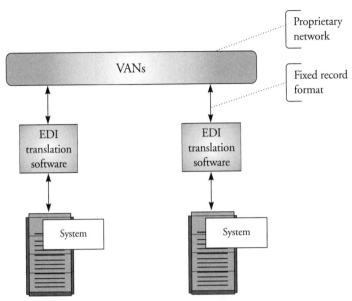

FIGURE 5.4 EDI using Value-Added Networks (VANs).

CORBA and DCOM were incompatible. In fact, early versions of the CORBA specification did not allow for interoperability among CORBA vendors. With time, however, CORBA became interoperable and CORBA/DCOM bridges became available to allow CORBA and DCOM to be interoperable.

Figure 5.5 shows the initial use of CORBA or DCOM. Using CORBA and DCOM for EDI at first involved a proprietary network and continued use of fixed record formats. The use of CORBA and DCOM simplified the development of EDI translation software because there was one of two standard transmission techniques. This allowed development of more packaged EDI translation software. As a result, the cost of entry for using EDI went down, but it was still out of reach for smaller companies.

One continuing problem with EDI was the use of fixed record formats. As shown on page 26 in Chapter 3, fixed record formats can create all sorts of processing problems which, in turn, increase maintenance costs, thereby driving up the costs of using EDI. XML was seen as a way to address this problem. The tagged structure of XML meant that the problem of sending the right data in the wrong record location—or sending the wrong data in the right record location—could be reduced significantly. This reduced errors and maintenance costs.

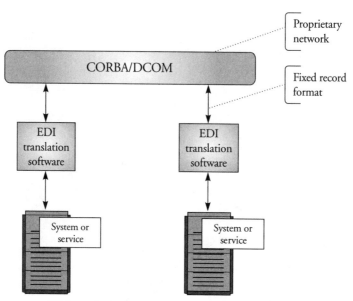

FIGURE 5.5   EDI initial use of CORBA or DCOM.

Figure 5.6 shows EDI use of XML with CORBA or DCOM. The rise of Internet connectivity by this time meant that proprietary networks could be replaced in some cases. Adapters for CORBA or DCOM could be used to transform the XML tagged record formats into the fixed record formats that internal EDI translations software would need. This effectively changed the problem of possible processing errors because of differing fixed record formats from one between organizations to one that is internal to an organization. The reason is that XML minimizes the possibility of those processing errors being propagated out to EDI partner organizations. The resilience of XML's tagged record format was explained in Chapter 3, starting on page 26.

Very shortly after XML came on the scene and was being considered for EDI standards, Web Services also showed up. Because Web Services also used XML, the shifting of EDI standards to Web Services was an obvious development. The initial immaturity of the Web Services specification restrained adoption, however. EDI needs both security and a transaction capability that were not in the initial Web Services specification. Nevertheless, the electronic business using eXtensible Markup Language (ebXML) initiative has been established by the United Nations Centre for Trade Facilitation and Electronic Business (UN/CEFACT) and OASIS[1] to research, develop, and pro-

---

1. More organizations working on standards related to Web Services can be found on page 191.

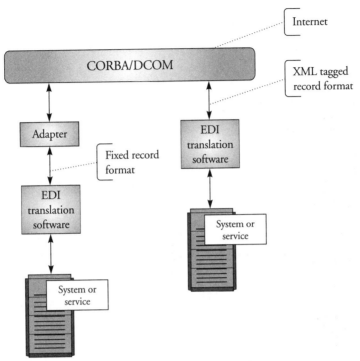

FIGURE 5.6 EDI use of XML with CORBA or DCOM.

mote global standards for the use of XML to facilitate the exchange of electronic business data. A major goal for ebXML is to produce standards that serve the same or similar purpose as EDI, including support for emerging industry-specific XML vocabularies.[2]

Figure 5.7 shows EDI use of Web Services. At first glance it looks quite similar to the EDI use of CORBA or DCOM in Figure 5.6. One difference, however, is the adapter that appears to the right in Figure 5.7. This is a Web Services adapter used by the service that appears below the adapter in Figure 5.7. This Web Services adapter is designed to work with this service. As a result, the EDI translation software can be eliminated. This further reduces maintenance costs. The use of Web Services also reduces the cost of entry into EDI for smaller organizations.

Of course, the world cannot change overnight. EDI will be in transition for a while. This is primarily because of existing installations of EDI that are presently working fine for many organizations. So, at first, industry-wide use

---

2. A sampling of industry-specific XML vocabularies can be found starting on page 212.

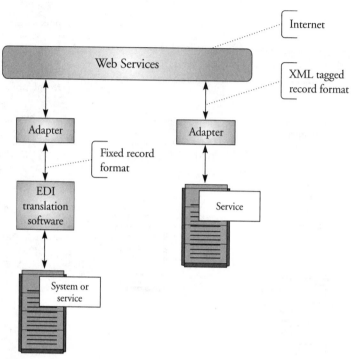

FIGURE 5.7 EDI use of Web Services.

of EDI will use all of the transmission and brokering techniques described so far. Figure 5.8 depicts how EDI will work in the transition period. Eventually, however, the nearly universal use of Web Services and resulting costs saving will drive EDI to a simpler model that will end up looking much like Figure 5.7.

Analysis of EDI

In Chapter 4, force field analysis was used to characterize driving and restraining forces affecting the adoption of various types of integration techniques. This analysis can also be applied to EDI as well. Figure 5.9 shows the major driving and restraining forces affecting the adoption of EDI.

The increasing use of EDI, product support of EDI, industry-standard definitions for EDI, and the availability of training and tools are all driving forces for the adoption of EDI. For smaller organizations, often one of the strongest driving forces is the requirement to adopt EDI in order to engage in business with larger organizations.

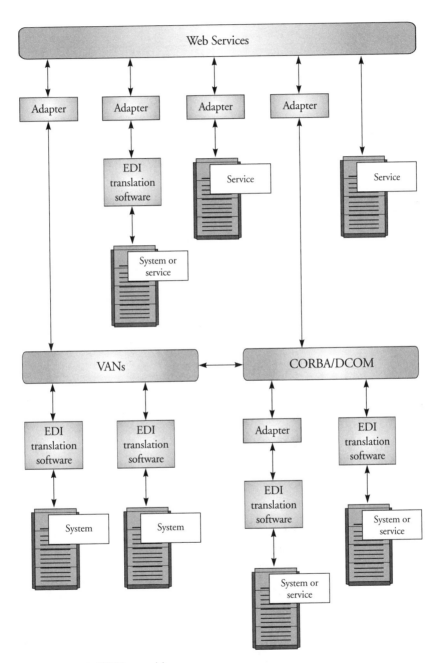

FIGURE 5.8 EDI in transition.

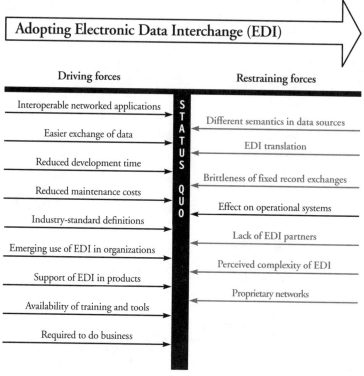

FIGURE 5.9 Force field analysis for adopting Electronic Data Interchange (EDI).

XML and Web Services address many of the restraining forces related to EDI. These include:

- Different semantics in data sources
- EDI or semantic translation
- Brittleness of fixed record exchanges (see page 26)
- Lack of industry-standard definitions

Web Services will also address the issue of proprietary networks for EDI. Proprietary networks can go away with Web Services since Web Services use HTTP (see page 225), which is virtually available everywhere because of the growth of the Internet. Assuming widespread adoption of Web Services and the attendant service-oriented architectures, the lack of trading partners will be reduced as a restraining force. Finally, the perceived complexity of EDI will be reduced by the perceived simplicity of Web Services.

When you look at Figure 5.9, the expansion and use of Web Services significantly reduces the strength of the restraining forces. These weakened restraining forces are shown in gray in the figure. Eventually, you are left with the impact EDI can have on operational systems, but this should be expected if up-to-the-moment processing is needed.

Evolutionary Use

Web Services and service-oriented architectures can be seen as evolution in process. Changes to our systems will start out incrementally and grow as people gain experience and standards evolve as well. Like any evolutionary process, there will also be competing forces. In this case, there will be competing products, standards, and ways of packaging services to name a few. It will likely be messy at times. Nevertheless, the way to win in this messy process is to wade in and participate.

Summary

Creating a Web site feature or to a custom portal is how most organizations will get started with Web Services. Using Web Services for business-to-business transactions is also rapidly gaining ground in many organizations. This chapter used the history of EDI as representative of the systems integration and data exchange issues any organization has had to address. Many organizations have gone through stages of internal integration and data exchange in much the same manner as described for EDI. But just as we have seen Web Services reducing the complexity and increasing the packaged system solutions for EDI, various forms of enterprise architectures will benefit in the same way. The next chapter looks at service-oriented architectures and enterprise architectures.

CHAPTER 6

Service-Oriented Architectures and Beliefs about Enterprise Architectures

A service-oriented architecture can be part of a wider enterprise architecture. In this chapter, we will look at beliefs about enterprise architectures and how a service-oriented architecture helps resolve some issues related to those beliefs. Beliefs about enterprise architectures have often been the reason that many attempts at implementing such enterprise architectures have fallen short of expectations. Some common beliefs are reviewed.

This chapter does not define a new way of developing enterprise architectures. It shows how aspects of a service-oriented architecture augment enterprise architecture methodologies and frameworks. An important point is how, within an enterprise architectural framework, certain beliefs can trip you up and how a service-oriented architecture can mitigate the effect of those beliefs. At the end of this chapter, there is a summary of the advantages of using service-oriented architectures as part of an enterprise architecture.

> ➤ "Function follows form,"
> Said Louis Sullivan one warm
> Evening in Chicago drinking beer.
> His wife said, "Dear,
> I'm sure that what you meant
> Is that form should represent
> Function. So it's function that should be followed."
> Sullivan swallowed
> And looked dimly far away
> And said, "Okay,
> Form follows function, then."

He said it again,
A three-word spark
Of modern arch-
Itectural brilliance
That would dazzle millions.
"Think I should write it down?"
He asked with a frown.
"Oh yes," she said, "and here's a pencil."
He did and soon was influential.[1]

Form Follows Function

"Form ever follows function" is the building architectural dictum credited to Louis Sullivan, the famous architect of the Chicago School of Architecture. This phrase, which has been used for building architecture, applies equally well to enterprise architecture. In this case, the "form" is the enterprise architecture. The "function" is the needs of the organizations that should be met by this architecture. We will see that this dictum applies equally well to using Web Services and a service-oriented architecture as part of an enterprise software architecture.

Service-Oriented Architecture as Part of an Enterprise Architecture

A service-oriented architecture is a part of an enterprise architecture and can be viewed as a "sub-architecture" of an enterprise architecture. Service-oriented architectures existed before the advent of Web Services. Technologies such as CORBA and DCOM afforded the opportunity to create service-oriented architectures. Some organizations also developed their own connection and messaging capability that afforded the opportunity to create service-oriented architectures.

Yet, using Web Services with a service-oriented architecture differs from many preceding efforts at developing a service-oriented architecture. A service-oriented architecture using Web Services provides a degree of flexibility not afforded with previous attempts using CORBA and DCOM, for example. This flexibility makes service-oriented architectures more responsive to organizational needs when trying to cope with the general chaos of business today. Being able to cope well with business chaos is an important "function" of enterprise architectures.

---

1. Poem: "Mrs. Sullivan," by Garrison Keillor (*We are still married*, pg. 231, Viking Penguin, Inc., 1989. Used with Permission).

One difference with using Web Services for a service-oriented architecture is that there is an unprecedented use of Web Services connections in software products and technologies. Returning to the AV system analogy, using Web Services is the equivalent to all AV products using RCA connectors. Continuing the analogy, using CORBA or DCOM were as if some AV components used coaxial connectors, some used RCA connectors, and some used both. Actually, for the analogy to be complete, you would have to say many also used neither coaxial nor RCA connectors. This is because there were many software products that simply did not work with CORBA and DCOM. It is difficult to build a comprehensive service-oriented architecture if there is spotty adherence to the way services can be connected. Using Web Services clears the way to build such a comprehensive service-oriented architecture.

Also, using Web Services makes it much easier to adhere to the "form follows function" dictum. To that end, designing service-oriented architectures will eventually be more like determining how to assemble an AV system that will also have some special equipment. For example, if I wanted to upgrade my AV system so that it would be as flexible as it could be, I would add a personal computer (PC) to the system. Figure 6.1 shows such a system. Assuming the PC has enough disk space, I would be able to store music from all my CDs, cassettes, and my older LPs. It could also store music I obtained from the Internet via the telephone or high-speed connection. I could then buy or build some software that would allow me to create various music programs that I could then route through the receiver. That software might also provide ways to classify my music, or to even share some of the music with others on the Internet. Using a PC, what I could do with that music is primarily limited to my imagination. Nevertheless, I could still add other components

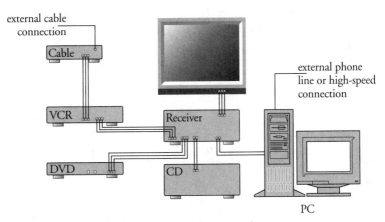

FIGURE 6.1 Audio-visual components with a personal computer.

such as a Digital Video Recorder or upgrade my receiver without affecting existing components or my PC. Many medium-sized and larger organizations can create an analogous architecture for their internal systems and services. They will buy and assemble most of their services, and add value by developing a service or some part of a service that gives their organization a competitive edge.

Just having Web Services for making connections, however, does not guarantee your organization will have a functional service-oriented architecture. There are design methods that should be used.

Service-Oriented Architectures with Architectural Frameworks and Methodologies

There are many methodologies and frameworks for developing enterprise architectures.[2] Such methodologies and frameworks usually describe an enterprise architecture in views, abstractions, or models. A common high-level abstraction is a conceptual business model where business processes and workflows are described.[3] A service or operational model is placed below the business model. This is where service functions or operations are defined to support the business model. Below the service or operational model is a system model that has logical data models and application architectures to support the service functions or operations. Some frameworks have additional models, but the important idea is that there are these layers or abstractions that aid in understanding an enterprise architecture. Frameworks are an excellent way of taking a holistic view of an enterprise architecture.

Service-oriented architectures add capabilities to layers or abstract models used in frameworks and methodologies. In Part III, an architecture will be presented that supports the use of these abstract models.

There are, however, common beliefs that can cause problems with the execution and understanding of any methodology. We will examine some of those beliefs.

---

2. Probably one of the best-known frameworks is the Zachman Framework for Enterprise Architecture. For more information on the Zachman framework, see www.zifa.com.

3. Some standards in this area include the Business Process Execution Language for Web Services (BPEL4WS), Business Process Modeling Language (BPML), Business Process Query Language (BPQL), and Business Process Specification Schema (BPSS). See pages 220–221 for more information.

Beliefs that Can Cause Function to Follow Form

As in any human endeavor, it is our beliefs that often shape the outcome. In the case of enterprise architecture, there are some common beliefs that have caused the implementation of the architecture to fall short of expectations.

Unfortunately, in many cases these beliefs can distort an enterprise architecture to the point where "function follows form." In other words, the form (or enterprise architecture) dictates what an information technology (IT) group can or cannot do to respond to the functional needs of the organization.

The following sections discuss some erroneous beliefs about enterprise architectures. These are provided so that you can be aware of the misconceptions when considering an enterprise architecture. Also, each section discusses the ways in which a service-oriented architecture can offset the effect of the misconceptions.

Building Architecture Analogies

Belief Creating an enterprise architecture is a lot like creating an architecture for a building.

Because I have already invoked the "form follows function" dictum of building architecture, it might seem odd that I would see a problem with the belief that creating an enterprise architecture is like creating the architecture for a building.

The problem with this belief is that it is taken far too literally. People would like to create the equivalent of a blueprint for a building's architecture. A building architecture is a detailed endeavor to create a structure that is meant to stand for many years. As a result, the drawings for a building are tremendously detailed. Likewise, people would like to create similarly detailed "drawings" for enterprise architectures.

Well, perhaps I am uniquely positioned to tell you that enterprise and building architectures simply cannot be compared. I have done both. As an undergraduate student, I studied building architecture and now, many years later, I have practiced as an enterprise architect.

Enterprise architectures need to be far more flexible than building architectures. For a building architecture to be as flexible as an enterprise architecture, you need to be able to change the floor plan of any floor, change where the stairwells and elevators go, add and remove whole floors, and expand and shrink the footprint of the building. So, if we go about creating rigid structures for our enterprise architectures, we end up forcing our functions to fit that form. These rigid structures can take several forms.

One such rigid structure might be to create separate systems that use a "foundation" of a shared database. The shared data model in such an enterprise architecture is often compared to the wiring or plumbing diagram in building architecture. Figure 6.2 depicts such a shared database architecture. In this figure, several different systems have direct access to a single database. The foundation of the database service is an agreed upon set of data elements to be used by all systems. What happens if an organization needs to make a significant change to its Customer Relationship Management (CRM) efforts? What if the change is too significant for the internal IT group to make right away? Furthermore, what if there is a commercial CRM package that supports the organization's requirements? Deciding to buy the package causes the CRM data to be divorced from the rest of the database. This lack of data integration may hamper the decision making process of the organization. Deciding not to buy the package means the organization needs to limp along until the internal IT group can make the changes to the CRM system. Any delays may mean the organization lost an important opportunity in the marketplace. In this example, the form (or shared database enterprise architecture) dictates what an IT group can or cannot do to respond to the functional needs of the organization.

Of course, any enterprise architecture needs a design of some sort. It is important, however, to not let the analogy of building architecture restrict how you might look at this design. Obviously, the analogy that I think works best is one of an AV system.

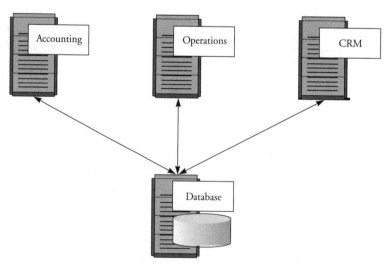

FIGURE 6.2 Shared database architecture.

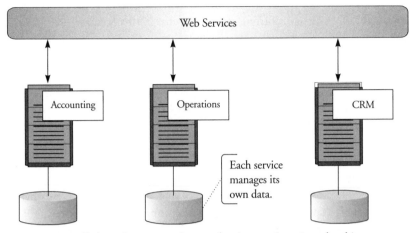

FIGURE 6.3 Each service manages its own data in a service-oriented architecture.

One aspect of a service-oriented architecture is that each service must manage its own data. Figure 6.3 illustrates this. Compare this figure to the previous one. Note that there is a disk underneath each service representing the data managed by the service. In addressing the example of replacing a CRM system described earlier, this architecture makes it much easier for an organization to respond to changing CRM needs. All the services in Figure 6.3 are not wired together by the underlying data model. Nevertheless, issues in how these services exchange data need to be addressed. That will be covered further in Part III.

Strategic Information and Day-to-Day Operations Alignment

Belief It is important that an enterprise architecture be aligned with both strategic information requirements and day-to-day operational data requirements.

I have found this statement in multiple enterprise architecture plans. It sounds good. In fact, who could argue with it? Nevertheless, the effect on the development of an enterprise architecture can be disastrous.

Anyone given this goal will obviously need to determine the strategic information requirements and the day-to-day operational data requirements. It is easy to get caught in "analysis paralysis" when doing this. I know. I have been there. Besides all the requirements and associated data needs that must be collected, this opens the opportunity for people to complicate matters by resisting the change in subtle ways. (We will cover that resistance in Part II of this book.) Between the mountain of analysis and the all-too-common mountain of resistance, nothing really happens. In this example, the form (or the analysis and resistance) holds back and sometimes dictates what an IT group can or cannot do to respond to the functional needs of the organization.

Of course, you need to take into account the strategic information requirements and the day-to-day operational data requirements in an enterprise architecture. But frankly, you don't need to get every single one of them documented. In fact, it might surprise you to find out that often existing software packages and services do already take into account most of these requirements. Strategic information requirements and operational data requirements do not vary that much among organizations. Nevertheless, where there is a special need in your organization, a service-oriented architecture allows you to isolate the software development needed for that special need from the more common services used by many organizations.

Data Conflict Resolution

Belief   The data in an enterprise architecture model cannot contain homonyms, synonyms, or other data definition conflicts.

This belief is often couched in terms of people throughout an organization using terms such as "customer" or "account," but when analyzed it becomes apparent that the terms "customer" and "account" mean different things to different parts of the organization.

Of course, most people realize that a single interpretation of "customer" or "account" will not work because there are very good reasons for the different meanings in different parts of the organization. What some people are now advocating, however, is to resolve any conflicting meanings so that the enterprise architecture not only provides the organization's overall definition of customer, but also reflects the various definitions understood and used by every enterprise element. Usually, it is advocated that there should be links between every enterprise architecture data element and every application data element that implements it. This is hard to argue against, but like the last belief, it results in "analysis paralysis" for many of the same reasons: a mountain of analysis and a possible mountain of resistance. As in the previous example, the form (or the analysis and resistance) holds back and sometimes dictates what an IT group can or cannot do to respond to the functional needs of the organization.

Even if the initial analysis was completed, what happens as soon as the organization acquires packaged software that uses a new definition of customer or account? Are all the links between every enterprise architecture data element in the newly acquired software then linked with the master documentation? Very few organizations will succeed in keeping this documentation up to date. Over time, it will be just as if no one had done the analysis in the first place. Documentation is important, but what is more important is realizing what the correct level of documentation is for your organization.

Nevertheless, it is important to be able to deal with data definition conflicts. They naturally exist. The Universal Business Language effort described on page 213 is one approach that appears promising as part of Web Services.

Common Issues with Many Enterprise Architectural Efforts

The overriding issue with most attempts at an enterprise architecture is an inherent lack of flexibility. Today's organizations need flexibility more than anything else. They need to be flexible to quickly move into new markets, develop completely new marketing campaigns, change how they work with their customers, acquire organizations, divest parts of the organization, and so on. Some attempts at enterprise architectures have, as an unfortunate and unintended consequence, reduced that flexibility. This section will cover such issues as analysis paralysis, over-standardization, and rigidity in data definition.

Analysis Paralysis

As mentioned previously, analysis paralysis often means that enterprise architectural effort really does not get off the ground. If the analysis is completed, it often ends up tremendously complicated and is not used. Nevertheless, applications are still built and software packages are acquired. The result all too often, is an inflexible "architecture" that does not serve the organization.

Over-Standardization

Once an organization reaches a certain size, there is simply a limit to the level of standardization that is possible. Different parts of the organizations have different needs. Imposing too many standards will either cause a lack of needed application development or will effectively cause a rebellion resulting in "stovepipe" development for particular parts of the organization which is effectively no integration.

Rigidity in Data Definition

Making data definitions too rigid is one form of over-standardization. Frankly, most organizations are going to acquire more software than build software. This means accepting the data definitions in that software and coming up with a flexible way to work with those definitions. Requiring any specific data definitions in software packages essentially precludes many software packages that might have otherwise been helpful to the organization.

Sometimes Enterprise Architectures Get Watered Down

Sometimes, just to be able to say that an organization has an enterprise architecture, the needs of the architecture get watered down. Here is a set of statements that were shared among several enterprise architecture documents I have seen. They express the goals of an enterprise architecture:

- Adopt industry standards.
- Use commercial off-the-shelf software as much as possible.
- Encapsulate legacy applications with interfaces that meet industry standards.
- Use a data independent layer between applications and data to hide the structure of the underlying data.

Again, who can argue with the statements? But there is no meat. For example, which industry standards or standard interfaces? An architecture needs to be specific but not rigid.

Goals of a Service-Oriented Architecture Using Web Services

The watered-down goals can be made more specific when considering a service-oriented architecture using Web Services. A specific, but not rigid set of goals could include:

- **Adopt industry standards.** These standards include Web Services and industry standard element definitions for XML. (The industry group specifying the standard element definitions could also be identified.[4])

---

4. A sampling of vocabularies by industry can be found starting on page 212.

- **Use commercial off-the-shelf software as much as possible.** The software must provide Web Services adapters.

- **Encapsulate legacy applications with interfaces that meet industry standards.** Web Services must be used for the interface.

- **Use a data independent layer between applications and data to hide the structure of the underlying data.** All interaction must be through Web Services.

Advantages of Service-Oriented Architectures

The main advantage for using a service-oriented architecture as part of an enterprise architecture is that it fits in with the general chaos of business. The "form" of an architecture must follow the "function," which is this general chaos of business.

In today's business environment there are many forces contributing to this chaos. Organizations are acquired and divested. Organizations restructure themselves. New products need to be sold. Competition forces quick responses. This list could be nearly endless. I am sure you can think of additional forces that could add to the chaos of business.

Historically, it is a struggle for the IT groups to respond to this business chaos. A service-oriented architecture provides a way to be more nimble in the responses. If a service-oriented architecture is designed properly, it will approach the type of plug-compatibility that I have been alluding to with the AV examples that I have sprinkled through this part of the book. Just like in your AV system, if you want a better DVD player, you can buy one and incorporate it fairly quickly into your AV system. Similarly, if your organization needs a new CRM system to respond to an unforeseen business need, you should be able to buy one and, with relative ease, integrate it into your existing service-oriented architecture. The trick, however, is how you design your service-oriented architecture.

Summary

A service-oriented architecture as part of an enterprise architecture:

- Permits your IT group to be more responsive to the needs of your organization.

- Reduces development costs because you will be able to use more packaged software.

- Reduces maintenance costs because you will be using more packaged software.

- Minimizes the costs of integrating systems because of the broad adoption of Web Services as an integration technique.

- Allows many smaller organizations to participate in Electronic Data Interchange (EDI).

Of course, you cannot instantly have a full-blown service-oriented architecture. The next chapter discusses the stages of adoption for Web Services and service-oriented architectures.

CHAPTER 7

Starting to Adopt a Service-Oriented Architecture

The remainder of this book will focus on the "sub-architecture" of a service-oriented architecture. This chapter provides an approach to adopting Web Services and service-oriented architectures along with a vision of the future using standardized services. At the end, a case is made for getting started with Web Services sooner rather than later.

➤ Continuing with my AV system analogy, the adoption of Web Services will be much like people treat their music collections. You start out with your own CDs and perhaps some cassette tapes. Commonly people make copies for their own use. They might load the music onto a hard drive and burn their own CDs to use in the car or elsewhere. This would be analogous to your internal development of services. At some point, you and a friend may exchange burned CDs. This would be analogous to a limited exchange with an external service. If you are really into music exchange, however, you are likely to get involved with Internet music file sharing at some point. This would be analogous to integrated exchanges with external services—much like the story of C. R.'s business trip. Many medium-sized and most larger organizations will go through these stages of adoption of a service-oriented architecture. (Actually, this AV analogy does not fully realize the flexibility of a service-oriented architecture. To be as flexible as a service-oriented architecture, an AV system would need to support an integrated music experience. For example, you start playing a CD, then a live band takes over to play a few bars, followed by a video of the band picking up the tune, all at the same time the score of the text is streamed to your monitor showing the notes being played.)

All Web Services Connections Look the Same

By now, you probably have noticed that all the Web Services connections in the figures tend to look the same. In fact, the Web Services protocols for connecting internal services are no different than the protocols needed for connecting internal services to external services. This explains the blurring of internal and external services mentioned on page 21 in the story of C. R.'s business trip. With Web Services and the pervasiveness of HTTP connections, it will become relatively easy to connect internal and external services together into service-oriented architectures. The rest of this chapter will attempt to give a flavor of what might be possible with this level of connectivity.

The Impact of Web Services

The initial impact that Web Services will have is to make existing forms of integration simpler. This will cause more organizations to be interested in the integration opportunities available with Web Services. Those opportunities may occur within an organization or between organizations.

The story of C. R.'s business trip illustrates some examples of what Web Services and a service-oriented architecture could mean for all of us. In addition to connectivity and integration, we can expect that businesses will find opportunities to provide services such as Customer Relationship Management (CRM) and Enterprise Resource Planning (ERP) on a subscription basis and that they will be integrated[1] with internal systems. (This is the blurring of internal and external services.) Automated agents that handle travel arrangements and help us manage calendars are also very likely. Also, devices that some might consider as nontraditional will be able to participate in Web Services. The example in C. R.'s business trip is the GPS assistant automatically receiving itineraries.

The opportunity for integration presented by Web Services will make using Web Services a requirement. The software products affected will range from desktop systems to distributed enterprise systems. It is highly probable, for example, that organizations of all sizes will find it economical to participate in a Web Services-based EDI system. This will most likely be driven by the accounting software packages. With EDI being based on the interconnec-

---

1. With Web Services, it is sometimes difficult to come up with the correct descriptive phrases. "Integrated" is not exactly the best term since the services are provided in a seamless way at many locations on the Internet. Another phrase might be "virtually integrated," but not everyone would immediately understand what is meant by "virtual." Eventually, we will have an agreed upon term for the type of "integration" allowed by Web Services. For now, however, I will use the term "integrated" in this book.

tivity of the Internet because of Web Services, anyone's accounting system should be able to participate. This could be extended to other types of packaged software as well.

The Internet Will Help Drive Adoption

The problem with predicting how service-oriented architectures will affect our systems is that the effect is not always immediately apparent. In some ways, it is fair to compare Web Services to the Internet in how it will affect many things we all do. For example, when the Internet was first developing, not many people predicted such uses as music file sharing, the explosion of genealogy data online,[2] or that grandparents would get personal computers to exchange e-mail messages with their grandchildren. Web Services constitute a similar situation in that people will think of all sorts of new and creative ways to use the capability.

The story of C. R.'s business trip is just one vision of how Web Services might change our world. It points out how everything boils down to connections and services to make a service-oriented architecture that can be assembled and reassembled much like an AV system.

Another way to look at C. R.'s business trip is to see the importance of the Internet in this service-oriented architecture. The prevalence of HTTP connections all over the world will make Web Services very enticing to developers to create all sorts of creative services that in turn, will make adoption of a service-oriented architecture an offer few businesses can afford to refuse.

Stages of Adoption for Web Services and Service-Oriented Architectures

Most organizations will go through the following stages of adoption for Web Services and service-oriented architectures:

1. **Experiment with Web Services.** This is a period to experiment with Web Services to become familiar with Web Services at a development level. The experimentation could involve adding external Web Services to a Web site or portal, having an application server access a single existing system using Web Services, or adapting two existing systems to exchange data using Web Services. As a result of experimentation, you will have a

---

2. The use of the Internet has massively increased the interest in genealogy. I know, this is one of my hobbies. In fact, I have a "hobby site" that helps you find family trees online. Take a look at www.familytreesearcher.com to see how much genealogy information is actually available.

better understanding of the concepts of Web Services, development tools, and the effectiveness of various training services.

2. **Adapt existing systems to use Web Services.** This will make it easier to use Web Services to "plug into" legacy systems. Many vendors have tools that make this adaptation easier. Some of the advantages were described in "Improving Internal Connections" on page 63.

3. **Remove intersystem dependencies.** These dependencies are along the line of shared databases that can restrict the flexibility of a service-oriented architecture described in "Building Architecture Analogies" on page 79.

4. **Establish an internal service-oriented architecture.** This will involve design to determine the appropriate boundaries of each service in your architecture. The techniques for this will be described in Part III.

5. **Expand the internal service-oriented architecture to include external services.** This actually could occur at any time that it seems appropriate to include external services. A simple early use would be to include external services in a portal as illustrated in "Improving Web Site Connections" on page 62.

Essentially, with these stages of adoption, internal data interchanges are simplified and your organization gains expertise in Web Services, which positions it for taking advantage of new internal and external services as part of a service-oriented architecture.

Vision of the Future

The effect of Web Services and service-oriented architectures means we are going to have fewer people involved in IT. The jobs in IT will also generally change to creating architectures and often realizing those architectures by making the connections to packaged services. At the same time, the quality of software will improve.

Industry will standardize on the capabilities of various services. An analogy was provided earlier to how the AV industry eventually settled on the capabilities of various AV components. The same will happen in every industry. As this happens, it will become easier to buy services and hook them together. We will have fewer and fewer people building custom software.

Continuing with the AV analogy, when many television manufacturers were first starting to convert to printed circuit boards, Zenith ran a series of ads promoting the fact that they still had people in their manufacturing plants who were hand-soldering electronic components for their television sets. Well, those handcrafted days are gone. Many of the traditional programming jobs will go the same way.

Some organizations may find that they have unique services that they can provide. IT staff will be needed to create those services. Nevertheless, there will be fewer jobs involving custom development.

With the eventual standardization of services, it will become easier to replace one packaged service with another. (This would be similar to replacing one AV receiver component with another that has more capabilities.) This should be a clarion call to software vendors to improve the quality of their product. There will be fewer reasons for organizations to put up with inferior software products if it is easy to swap in a service from a different vendor. Plug-compatibility means that services can be replaced easily.

Why Get Started Now?

There seems to be an opinion held by some that is there is no need to look at Web Services until you have another organization as a partner for exchanging business data. Although that may be true for very small organizations, it is not true for many other organizations. Do not assume that Web Services are simply for exchanging data with other organizations. No, Web Services are about connections. And you can make those connections in your own organization.

Of course, for very small organizations, you may need to wait until the vendors or your accounting system or contact manager provide a way for you to take advantage of Web Services.

For medium sized to larger organizations, applying the concepts and standards of Web Services to your internal systems serves two purposes. First, it is a means to simplify your internal data interchanges. Second, it allows your organization to gain expertise in Web Services. Should the opportunity present itself, your organization might then be able to provide a service to other organizations and/or your organization might be able to take advantage of services provided by other organizations.

The message is that if you have not prepared yourself, you won't be ready when the opportunity shows up.

Summary

Service-oriented architectures that use Web Services will result in a blurring between internal and external services. Architectures will be constructed using a combination of those internal and external services. As time goes on, these services will become more standardized making it easier to replace one "plug-compatible" service with another. The result will be competition to create higher quality software in these services.

To take advantage of the services that are starting to become available, it is important to get started in the short term. The adoption of service-oriented architectures using Web Services, however, will be a big change for most organizations. The next part of this book will examine some issues related to managing this change.

Managing Change Needed for a Service-Oriented Architecture

Moving to a service-oriented architecture will be a significant change for many organizations. Such change must be managed properly, which involves considering the organization as a whole, the technology to be used, and the people involved in the change. Part II provides ideas to consider in managing the change needed to create a service-oriented architecture.

CHAPTER 8

Change Will Happen

This chapter is about managing the change that will occur with adopting a service-oriented architecture that uses Web Services. It shows that as the technical issues diminish, the remaining restraining forces are business issues, design issues, and change issues. This chapter primarily deals with change issues. These issues most often will manifest themselves in resistance to change. Forms of resistance are discussed as well as ways to overcome such resistance. To anchor these concepts of resistance, I have included some of my own experiences with resistance to change.

At the end of this chapter, there is a worksheet for laying out change issues and responses to those issues. There is also a consolidated force field analysis for adopting a service-oriented architecture that builds on the analyses covered in Chapter 4.

➤ After completing my undergraduate work, I had a job as an analyst in a government agency. This was in a research group of about 40 people. One day a senior analyst decided to move some of the desks around and, without discussing it with the people involved, went right ahead with the move. Orville, one of the older analysts, was not there at the time. Orville came back to find his desk in a different spot. Finding out who made the change, Orville ran screaming at the senior analyst and literally pushed him against the wall. As it turned out, Orville had an emotional problem that meant he did not deal with change well at all. The senior analyst, however, could have avoided this confrontation if only he had spoken with Orville before making the changes.

Change

Not everyone who has problems dealing with change has emotional problems that make transitions worse. In fact, most of us deal with change better than Orville did in this true story. Nevertheless, there are ways to make any change easier for people and for the organization. This chapter deals with change related to Web Services and service-oriented architectures and ways to deal with that change.

We are on the cusp of a tremendous change in the way we develop and maintain technical systems in our organizations. This change is already in progress and it will be a watershed for the software industry and software development in general. The use of Web Services appears to be the missing puzzle piece in creating a complete picture of making a service-oriented architecture work. This manifests itself by the almost universal adoption of Web Services by software vendors and by the rapid introduction of new products to make it easier to connect legacy systems to Web Services.[1]

Costs Related to Adopting a Service-Oriented Architecture

The stages of adoption of a service-oriented architecture were discussed in Chapter 7. Each stage will lead to different changes occurring in organizations. The stages are repeated here, but this time with a discussion of the types of costs that will likely occur:

1. **Experiment with Web Services.** This will usually involve only a few people on short projects in order to become familiar with Web Services at a developmental level. The costs here will involve training, perhaps the purchase of some software tools, and the time to experiment with using Web Services.

2. **Adapt existing systems to use Web Services.** Depending on your internal architectures, this stage may mean more work for the IT group. It will mean acquiring or building Web Services adapters for existing systems. That process will require additional expenditures in either training of internal personnel or bringing in people to do the work.

---

1. Of course, not every vendor is embracing Web Services. Some do not want their systems to be so open, accessible, or replaceable. Market forces, however, are going to be irresistible and at some point vendors will need to participate in Web Services in order to survive. Recall the analogy where Zenith was trying to counter the market forces on page 90. It didn't work.

3. **Remove intersystem dependencies.** If you have internal systems that should be separate services, but share database structures or other infrastructure, you may need to invest in removing these dependencies. Additional costs may include analyses to determine other intersystem dependencies that might restrict the construction of a service-oriented architecture. Of course, you do not need to bother with removing these intersystem dependencies if they do not conflict with building a service-oriented architecture.

4. **Establish an internal service-oriented architecture.** With intersystem dependencies removed, you can now establish an internal service-oriented architecture. At this point, costs will start to go down. Initially, this is because of the likely reduction in maintenance cost through the use of Web Services as the universal connection technology.

5. **Expand the internal service-oriented architecture to include external services.** Once you have a service-oriented architecture, you can start looking for "plug-compatible" software that can further reduce your development costs. It is at this point that you will start to see a significant reduction in costs since this is where the number of custom programming jobs starts to diminish. Chapter 7 covered the changing roles of IT staff in a service-oriented architecture. It is at this stage that an organization will see those changes occur.

Figure 8.1 provides a general view of costs over time related to adopting Web Services and a service-oriented architecture. The various curves are only projections meant to show that timing of costs rising and falling will vary based on the nature of an organization's existing internal systems architecture. In other words, "one size won't fit all."

> *While I was completing the final manuscript of this book, a friend who was not familiar with Web Services asked how anyone would make money using this technology. First, I discussed Web Services using the AV analogy. Then I said that one way to look at Web Services is that they are the connections between various services on the Internet much like cables are the connections between AV components. That made sense to him. So I said, there is obviously more money to be made on AV components than on the cables. The same is true for Web Services. There is more money to be made on the services provided using Web Services than on the Web Services technology itself.*

So, if anyone asks about the Return on Investment (ROI) for Web Services, it would be best to deflect the question. The real issue is the ROI on services that could be provided for a service-oriented architecture using Web

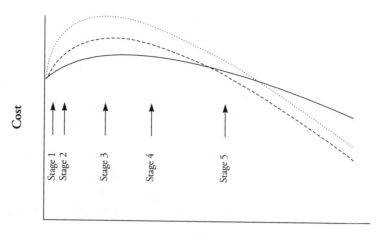

Time

FIGURE 8.1 Costs over time related to adopting Web Services and a service-oriented architecture.

Services. That is where the innovation will occur and where the real opportunity exists for making money. Web Services are just the connections.

Technical Change Issues Diminishing

As previously mentioned, there are several kinds of issues related to change. The drive to use Web Services is reducing the technical change issues. In other words, the barriers to change related to technology are diminishing. This makes moving to a service-oriented architecture technically easier.

Figure 8.2 shows how using Web Services affects adoption of a service-oriented architecture overall. This figure combines the force field analyses for three basic components of a service-oriented architecture: Web Services middleware (Figure 4.7), data warehousing (Figure 4.9), and message routing (Figure 4.14). The restraining forces shown at the right represent the technical change issues for all three components. The gray arrows represent the technical restraining issues that will diminish as industry adopts and expands the use of Web Services. Why these forces will diminish was discussed in Chapter 4.

The analysis in Figure 8.2 is interesting because it illustrates that as the technical restraining forces shown in gray diminish, we are left with technical issues related to business and general design. The arrows at the top, right, represent the business issues such as costs of development or concerns that a product or service doesn't have all the features that might be needed. The arrows at the bottom, right, represent the design issues. There are, of course,

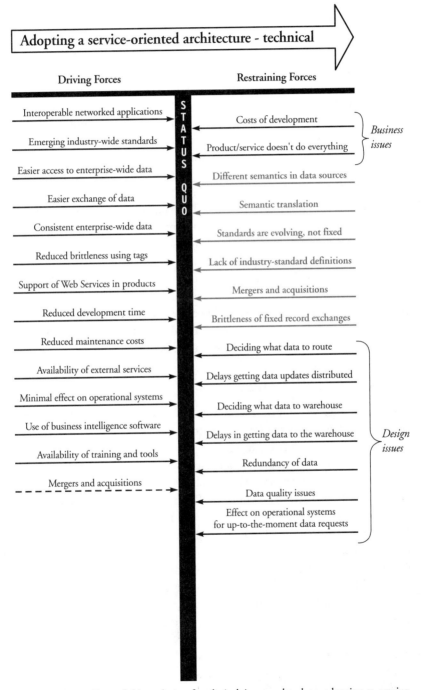

FIGURE 8.2 Force field analysis of technical issues related to adopting a service-oriented architecture.

other design issues, but these arrows are representative of basic design issues facing any effort to create a service-oriented architecture.

At the left of Figure 8.2 are the driving forces for adopting a service-oriented architecture using Web Services. The strength of these forces will vary by organization. Also, there very well might be additional driving forces for a particular organization. Nevertheless, by almost any measure, there are tremendous driving forces for the adoption of a service-oriented architecture.

You may want to try adding technical driving and restraining forces to this figure that are specific to your organization. There is space at the bottom of Figure 8.2 to add technical driving and restraining forces.

Figure 8.2 illustrates that there are few industry-wide technical issues remaining that restrain the adoption of service-oriented architecture and that those issues are diminishing over time. This is why you see the adoption of Web Services by software vendors and the introduction of new products to make it easier to connect legacy systems to Web Services.

This is not to diminish the business and design issues. They are not necessarily easy to solve, but they are the stuff of what developing an architecture is all about. Essentially, each organization must decide if it makes business sense to create a service-oriented architecture using Web Services. If it does, then there are design issues that need to be addressed. At this juncture in our industry, the common, industry-wide roadblocks are coming down.

Resistance to Change

If it makes sense for your organization to develop a service-oriented architecture, what other restraining forces need to be considered? Probably the strongest is a general resistance to change.

Resistance is a common human response to change. This human resistance to change, however, may very well be the biggest hurdle to overcome in creating a service-oriented architecture. The previous section showed how the use of Web Services has and will continue to reduce the technical restraining forces on the adoption of the technologies related to adopting service-oriented architectures. With the reduction in the technical restraining forces, change is certainly going to happen. As the technical issues recede, the human side of resistance to change is also going to happen.

Figure 8.3 shows the analysis of driving and restraining forces related to change that affect the adoption of a service-oriented architecture. There are many more restraining forces that relate to resistance to change. Also, if my vision of the future concerning the roles of IT staff in the future is correct, some of the restraining forces simply will be stronger. For example, the restraining force of feeling that jobs may be threatened is very real as an orga-

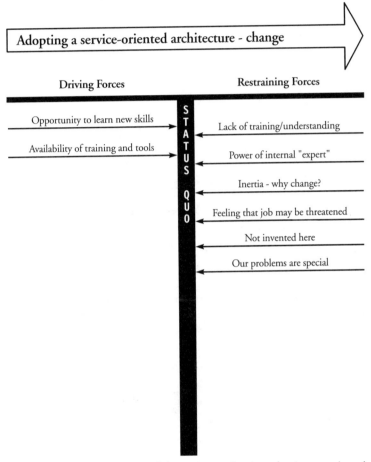

FIGURE 8.3 Force field analysis of change issues related to adopting a service-oriented architecture.

nization moves through the stages of adopting a service-oriented architecture. You may want to try adding driving and restraining forces to this figure that are specific to your organization. There is space at the bottom of Figure 8.3 to add driving and restraining forces.[2]

As a manager, be on the lookout for resistance. Where there is change, there will be resistance. The savvy manager is prepared for it and deals with it as it occurs. In reality, only about one fourth of people actually like change

---

2. Yes, many of these same forces have existed for the adoption of any technology for many years. Nevertheless, I think there is something seriously afoot with Web Services and that the expanding adoption of service-oriented architectures will have a significant impact on IT organizations.

and look forward to it. Those are the people who are looking for variety and they are your advocates in a technological change. There are probably an equal number of folks who hate change; these folks may try to keep change from happening. In the middle are the "wait and see" folks. They are concerned about the impact of change to them, but they are willing to wait and see what happens. These are the people to focus some time on because you can win them to your side. Plenty of communication and participation can do wonders. The more employees can worry and wonder, the stronger their resistance becomes. It's just human nature.

William Bridges has written extensively on the topic of change in organizations for the past several decades. His work, particularly *Managing Transitions*,[3] is particularly helpful for the manager planning a technology change. His model views change as a series of events going from an ending, which is the way things used to be, to a beginning, which is the way things will be in the future when the project is complete. Between the two is the neutral zone, which is a stage in which few things are the way they were and it's not clear how they will be.

It is in the neutral zone, according to Bridges, where resistance can be found because it is a stage that can be marked by confusion and uncertainty. In the neutral zone there are no clear markers and no promises. The savvy manager will be careful when dealing with people who may be in the neutral zone because they are seldom being difficult on purpose. They are unsure and concerned and may not realize their resistance. Sensitivity to the neutral zone is important because the manager can often help team members through this stage more quickly.

Forms of Resistance

Recognizing resistance can take some practice because many of its forms could easily be justified as a concern or a request for information. We all want employees who care enough about their work that they are willing to want to understand and state their concerns. As new projects are presented, it should be expected that employees would have many questions. In fact, one of the best things that a manager can do is communicate in many ways and many times what the project entails. Some employees do better with written communication, some with group meetings, and some with one-on-one casual conversations. All have their place in a plan for communicating change.

---

3. *Managing Transitions: Making the Most of Change,* William Bridges, 1991, Perseus Publishing, New York.

When a manager has communicated plans and time has passed, some team members may still be asking questions or raising concerns. Sometimes team members may be raising new concerns on a regular basis. If you have carefully considered the objections and found no grounds for the concern, this may well be a sign of resistance to change. Resistance to change in people can take many forms. Constant questioning with new concerns rising all the time is a classic sign that resistance may be taking place. This also can take the shape of a form of confusion, in which the team member just can't quite get clear on how or why the project will be the way it is planned. Such a team member is probably not doing this on purpose. It's possible that this person is just not able to hear what is being communicated because of some discomfort with it. This person may well be in the neutral zone and is just trying to find his or her way through it.

Other forms of resistance may include silence or easy acceptance. People may be silent for many reasons but it is easy to assume that silence means acceptance. That is not always the case, so be on the lookout for it. Easy acceptance can also be misleading because it may mean that the person has not considered the ramifications of the change; when he or she does think about it, you may find that this person upon whom you were counting is no longer on board.

The following sections go into some detail on forms of resistance. These forms of resistance will also be referenced in the remainder of this chapter, Chapter 9, and Chapter 10.

Lack of Training/Understanding

Sometimes people are resistant to change because they do not have the training to understand what the new project or job will entail. Many people become familiar with their job and want it to stay the same. It is particularly challenging for them if the change in their job involves new technology. Almost everyone has a concern about not measuring up in a new environment and that may well be the situation here.

A second issue in this situation is communication. Sometimes people just aren't getting the message that they need to hear. In a change situation, you can count on some people putting the most negative spin on any change. That's just human nature. In a time of uncertainty, most people will fear for the worst. That's why plenty of communication is of great importance. If people will need new training for the change, be sure they are reassured that they will get it.

Power of Internal "Expert"

An internal expert can be a formidable ally in a change effort or a formidable roadblock. Such an expert knows the current system and possibly the previous systems in such a way that can be of great help. On the other hand, if this person is not on board for the change effort, he or she can raise all sorts of barriers. The most probable form of resistance will be in raising concerns about the quality of the new system and this person is likely to use the expert position in the organization to raise the level of recognition of the concern.

It's easy to overlook what an expert has to lose in a change situation. This person is going from being an acknowledged success to a situation that is new. Because of the newness, it is impossible to know whether this person will be able to retain expert status or even if he or she will be needed in the new situation. That may be a big risk for such a person. This is especially true in the situation where the current expert may not have the kind of training that will make moving to the new system possible.

Inertia—Why Change?

Sometimes it's difficult to effect change in a system just because it's always been done a certain way or because the system is seen as working okay. This creates a sense of inertia. People who are part of the system ask why a change is needed. This can make it difficult when the new way of things will create a leap forward and will bring possibilities that haven't been present before. Communicating the advantages of the new options may help, but when people are comfortable in the current situation, any change can be challenging and bring resistance into play.

Feeling that Job May Be Threatened

Given the pace of technological change today, it is difficult for most people to stay knowledgeable on new technology. This means that any change may feel threatening to many people. Many technology changes are put into place so that staffing can be as lean as possible. That means that not everyone will have a job after the change in technology occurs. Those people who have not kept their technical skills up may have reason to worry. Because worry tends to be contagious in an organization, most everyone will be worrying. For some people, the outlet for this worry will be resistance.

As the use of Web Services is more widely adopted, some jobs will really be threatened. We are on the cusp of replacing custom coded systems with "plug-compatible" software. As a manager, you will need to keep this very legitimate concern in mind when creating a service-oriented architecture.

Not Invented Here

Most people have pride in their work. It's easy for managers to forget or not even know the blood, sweat, and tears that went into a project that was completed some time ago. The people who worked on that project do remember. When they hear that the work that they did will be replaced, there's always a sense of loss. In the excitement of bringing in the new, the organizational focus ignores the earlier contribution of the people and their project and focuses on the shortcomings of the old. This can lead to resistance on the part of those who have worked on the old system.

Our Problems Are Special

I've worked with countless groups of people working on technology issues. Amazingly, almost all of them believed that the technical problems that they had to solve were quite complex and unusual. From my perception as an outsider, those same problems struck me as fairly normal for the industry that they were in or the work that they were doing. There were, of course, some twists that required attention, but those twists were not significant enough to scuttle a project.

This is a common excuse used by technical people to avoid using an off-the-shelf program. On a rare occasion it may be true, but most often it is just a means of resistance used by those who want to keep things as they are or to develop something new on their own.

Overcoming Resistance to Change

The first step in overcoming any kind of resistance to change is to recognize it for what it is. Some resistance easily stops a project because it is never addressed. When the manager notices that nothing seems to be happening or that the project is far off the schedule, it's past time to consider that resistance is at play.

The best bet is to anticipate resistance in advance, even before the project starts. This means that you can set things up to avoid some of the resistance and you will be in a good situation to address it as it arises. Some ideas are listed here.

The next sections discuss ways to overcome resistance to change. These will be used in the remainder of this chapter.

Selecting the Right People

One key to the success of any project is careful selection of people to work on the project. Selecting a person because he or she has been around a long time isn't generally a good reason for that person to be on the team. Choosing someone because he or she doesn't currently have a project is not a good reason either. The best approach is to identify what kind of skills and experience are needed on the project team. Then figure out which person in your organization can meet those standards. What isn't available internally must be obtained externally either through a new hire or a contracting situation.

Sometimes staffing for a project is seen as a way to resolve problem personnel situations. That's not the route to success on your project. Although I've never seen any research on this, my experience tells me that a big factor in failed projects is a lack of personnel with the skills and experience required. This is something that will hinder any project. The outcome of any project can only be as successful as the skills of the people who work on it.

A Second Set of Eyes

Another practice that can be great help in limiting resistance is pairing team members together. There are many methodologies that call for paired team members. There are excellent technical reasons to do this, but there are reasons also that will address resistance to change. Careful team selection means that you are unlikely to have both people in the pair with the same issues. That means that neither person will be left stewing on his or her own. In addition, the possibility that both people will be allowing the schedule to slip or participate in other resistant activities is less likely.

Really Listen

One of the best things that you can do with someone whom you think may be experiencing resistance is to listen. By that, I mean really listen and not try to talk the person out of his or her ideas. Most of the time, what we think is listening is actually thinking about how to answer the person's objections. If you find yourself talking more than the other person, it means you aren't really listening. If you find yourself explaining things, then you aren't really listening.

Some people think that just saying the same thing over and over will help improve understanding. When you find yourself doing this, it means that you don't really understand what the person is saying. Sometimes what the person is saying is the problem is just the obvious surface of the real problem.

It's more effective to ask the other person questions to probe into what might be behind the resistance. Ask questions such as "what is your concern about that?" and follow up your questions with a summary such as "so, you are concerned that if we implement this change, _____ might happen and that would be a problem because of _____." Let the person clarify your understanding until you both agree that you understand the other person's point of view.

If you listen in this way, you can even disagree but the person will feel that he or she has been heard. People don't necessarily need agreement to feel that they've been heard.

Communicate at Many Levels

An effective antidote to resistance is communication and plenty of it. It's a human response to anticipate the bad things that may happen and a communication vacuum contributes to that.

To deal with resistance issues, regular communication in many forms is helpful. People have different styles and it's helpful to provide communication in as many forms as possible so that each style gets its needs met.

It also can be helpful to establish a communication schedule so that people can anticipate when more communication will be available to then. In fact, any promises that are made must be met. Don't overpromise and then not meet the promises. That just sets up a foundation for mistrust.

And while you're at it, think about communicating up the management chain as well. Find methods that will be reassuring to management and create a schedule that you can meet and that they can depend upon. This helps protect your project from rumor and innuendo.

Seek Appropriate Avenues to Involve People

Participation is another important part of avoiding resistance to change. The more people feel part of something, the more they will support it. This can take a variety of forms including asking for people's input and review. Be sure to be clear in your request for information so that people really hear the request and believe it is really wanted. I've seen situations where management asked for input and got none because employees either didn't hear it or didn't believe it. If asking for input is not a regular part of your organization's culture, you will need to ask in a variety of ways. Sometimes a casual request at the water cooler creates a more believable request than a general statement in an open meeting.

Get Resistance Out in the Open

Naming resistance for what it is can bring it out into the open so that people can talk about it. Talking about it takes away its power to disrupt.

It's important to do this in a neutral, nonthreatening way. That means that pointing a finger and telling a person or group that they are resisting change is not an option. That approach is quite likely to make things worse even if it is true. It's better to create a situation where people can state their resistance on their own. Hold a team meeting and create a comfortable situation by stating something like, "I'm sure you have concerns about this change. I'll bet that the new architecture is a little hard to understand in such a short time. At least I know I'd feel that way." Approaching the issue in this way would make it possible to get the issue on the table for discussion.

Some Resistance Scenarios

This section includes scenarios that are from some of my own experiences with resistance to change (of course, names and details have been altered). As you read the following scenarios, you will see certain themes emerging. The first is that resistance can take many forms and is not always immediately recognizable as resistance. The second is that the resister is often not even aware of the motivation for his or her behavior.

But It's So Complicated!

As he put a team together to replace an existing system, the manager felt fortunate to be able to include a person who had worked on the existing system for over a decade. Betty was a competent programmer and had a nearly encyclopedic memory of why the existing system worked the way it did. She was also quite articulate and seemed very interested in helping to create the replacement system.

The early investigations into how the replacement system should work went well. Betty was quite helpful in making sure the team had all the details and idiosyncrasies documented. She was also very helpful went it came to designing the data model the replacement system would use.

Then something happened. As the team started to design how the software would work, Betty started to bring up new issues that should have been uncovered in the early investigations. Of course, it is understandable that some things would be overlooked but the number of these issues became overwhelming. Sometimes, these issues required considerable rework to change what was already completed. It seemed as if Betty waited until all the rework was done before bringing up another issue. And unfortunately, sometimes these issues also required rework. Eventually, however, the team seemed to have a robust design and was able to answer many of Betty's concerns on the spot.

Then things started to get a bit weird. When team members would answer one of Betty's concerns and show her how the design took into account the issue she raised, Betty would often respond, "but it's so complicated." Betty was apparently convinced that the existing system had to be more complicated than the replacement system would be.

Because of her experience on the existing system, Betty had a huge following in this large organization. She was known and respected all the way up to the vice president level because she had worked with these people for over ten years. This replacement system was also seen as critical to the organization's future. So, when Betty started moving up the management chain with her lament, "but it's so complicated," people took notice. Management started to want to know why the group was doing this inferior design and became worried about the future of the project. In fact, some vice presidents started to threaten cancellation of the project if the information technology (IT) group could not do a better job on this critical replacement system. A lot of money was still allocated to completing this project and they did not want to spend that much money on an inferior replacement.

More and more time was spent on meetings with upper management. The system designers and analysts all had to attend numerous meetings. In those meetings, Betty brought up issue after issue concerning how much more complicated the existing system is compared to the proposed system. The dynamic was interesting. The issues Betty brought up were often in terms that management could understand. The explanation of how the proposed system would handle the issues often had to be in terms of data models and software architecture. Many people in management honestly did not understand the more technical explanations, so they were left with the impression that Betty might have a point.

Time passed. Development slowed. Eventually, the project was canceled. Some time later, a packaged product was brought in to replace the existing system. But as you might expect, Betty at first thought the packaged product would work only later to discover that the packaged product needed much modification, because the existing system was so "complicated." That project was also canceled.

Resistance Issues

- Lack of training/understanding
- Power of internal "expert"
- Inertia—why change?
- Feeling that job may be threatened
- Our problems are special

Every technical change has incredible impact on the people involved with both the new and old systems. In fact, every change of this type has winners and losers. As development proceeds, people sometimes change camps.

In this scenario, Betty had worked hard over the years with the current system. She was incredibly bought into it and very impressed with how well it worked and how important her role was. Because of her years of experience, she had created a strong network of personal advocates for her point of view. Initially, she may have been sure that no new system could possibly replace the system that she knew was very complicated, so she was willing to work on the team to replace it. In fact, she had already been on several committees in the past that had put the kibosh on replacements because the existing system, and of course, the work that it had to do, was so complicated. In this particular situation, she was willing to participate and cooperate on the team until it dawned on her that this replacement system might actually happen. Then she began to raise issue after issue. When this happened, it's apparent that on some level she had begun to feel challenged in her position as the resident expert. The rest is history. She used all of her connections to stop this project. Upper management can be notoriously fearful of failure and Betty's concerns fed right into that. Sometimes it may seem that anybody can kill a project because of any "issue" while it's very hard to get enough people or the right people to back it.

Suggestions to Overcome Resistance

- Really listen
- Communicate at many levels
- Seek appropriate avenues to involve people
- Get resistance out in the open

The most important issue in this scenario is to recognize the people issues that come with change. This has implications both with the people doing the work and management that has to support the work.

Technical people generally approach others in the organization—and questions within the IT organization—from a technical perspective. While technical questions must have technical answers, there are other issues at stake that, left unanswered, will sink a project. In this case, Betty's issues were not technical. They were personal. The closer implementation came, the nearer she was to losing her standing as the resident expert. So, naturally, the old system, her system, became more and more complicated and irreplaceable. From the start, listening to Betty was important, but, beyond that, finding an important role for her in the new project was critical. Because she had connections in upper management, perhaps she could have served as communication person in the project and an implementation role for the replacement system would have been important. The new system would have required training for employees, which might have been a good spot for her.

Now, granted, finding the right role might be challenging and might require some coaching or mentoring to get her up to speed, but the alternative, in this case, was a failed project.

A second issue in this case, is getting management on board. In this case, Betty was able to cancel a project through a whisper campaign to her old buddies in management. This indicates that management was not properly briefed or brought on board at the beginning of the project, nor was it kept on board during development. This is another situation where technical people may oversell the technical answer and not carefully communicate, on a regular basis, the information that can be understood. The very technical answers that can be so important and interesting to technical people may put off management that does not understand their significance. This means learning to go beyond the technology to what the technology will do for the organization. What are the outcomes that will make a difference to them? This should be the focus of technical/management discussions. When this occurs, a project will be less vulnerable to a whisper campaign.

Guerilla Tactics

One of the best technical minds in the company, Nancy was given the responsibility of designing and implementing the integration of two systems critical to her organization. The integration was somewhat controversial, with some seeing it as necessary and others thinking it the wrong direction. Nancy stated that she was in favor of the integration and was given the responsibility for completing the project. She put together a small team and set to work on the problem. To many in the organization, this seemed to be about a 2-month project. Nancy concurred.

At the 2-month point, the project was not done. Nancy assured everyone that it was well on its way. At 4 months, it was still not done. Again, Nancy said that it was being properly handled; there were just a few glitches. At 7 months, a contract was missed and the project was canceled.

Resistance Issues

- Power of internal "expert"
- Inertia—why change?

What happened? Turns out that Nancy really enjoyed working on the fringes of technology. She found some academic research that seemed to fit this problem quite well. Her team enjoyed working on the fringes of technology as well. They put together quite an elegant plan that involved writing significant amounts of code. Never mind that you could buy portions of the solution. Hooking that into the full solution would be less elegant. Given her status in the company, little oversight was maintained on any work she did.

What really happened? Although she had stated that she supported the integration project, Nancy did not think it was the right direction for her company. She may not have even been aware that she was using her emphasis on the elegant solution as a way to kill the project, but that's what happened. Resistance is an emotional reaction that can leave people unaware of the motivations for their actions.

Suggestions to Overcome Resistance

- Selecting the right people
- A second set of eyes
- Seek appropriate avenues to involve people
- Get resistance out in the open

Managing brilliant, creative people has been a challenge since management began. Harnessing that capability in a way that will benefit the organization can be overwhelming. In this particular case, Nancy either was not the right person for the job or she was not managed properly.

Selecting the right people for the tasks in a technology project may be the most critical decision, but it is often less studied than the hardware and software to be used. Nancy's interest in the fringes of technology can be very helpful to a company, but in this case, it killed a critical, yet constrained, 2-month project. Her management should have foreseen this problem and could have either had someone else head the project or paired Nancy with someone who could steer her brilliance in a more pragmatic direction.

Second, Nancy and her organization were unaware of her true feelings about this project. Managers need to be on the lookout for signs of resistance. When things just don't add up, resistance may be in play. Managers need to assess how things are going and be ready to make changes.

Nancy's manager should have taken a closer look at the project on an ongoing basis. Checking in at 2 months, when the project was to have been completed, was too late. Using standard project management techniques, a detailed schedule should have been developed and checkpoints, perhaps on a weekly basis, should have been observed. Design walkthroughs, code reviews, or inspections might also have helped. Given Nancy's interest in the fringe of technology and her possible resistance, these checkpoints should have been quite in depth. This would have flagged the slowing schedule early on and changes could have been made.

More Guerilla Tactics

Todd had almost single-handedly built the company's master record system. In fact, he had also been involved in the construction of two successive generations of the master record system. Like Betty, he had the respect of nearly everyone in the company. Only in this case, that respect was so high that he was seen as a system guru. Todd agreed that it was once again time to upgrade the master record system. The present system was not fast enough and cost too much to maintain. Todd saw this as an opportunity to improve on his previous designs.

What Todd had built, however, was now available from numerous software vendors. Some of those vendors could legitimately show that their packaged software products could significantly outperform the system that Todd had designed. A technical review of the capabilities of the packaged software products showed, to most everyone's satisfaction, that the software could perform as needed. But not for Todd. In meetings, he often brought up arcane issues. When asked to document them, he agreed. But it never happened and given his standing in the organization, his lack of follow-through was never mentioned. More meetings would bring more concerns. To everyone on the development team, it was becoming clear that Todd had never been satisfied with the master records systems he had designed and that he wanted one more chance to do it "right." The packaged software option would take away his opportunity.

Todd and the CEO of the company were close friends and had been with the company from its start. Eventually, this relationship allowed Todd to recreate his master record system. It may not surprise you that the new system is still not as fast as the packaged system and requires more maintenance.

Resistance Issues

- Not invented here
- Power of internal "expert"
- Feeling that job may be threatened
- Our problems are special

This scenario illustrates a huge change that has already occurred in the software business. Not that many years ago, most organizations had to rely on a system guru and a large staff inside the organization that could design unique applications to meet the organization's unique needs. Now many software vendors have products that can be used as is or be tweaked to meet the organization's needs. This is a huge opportunity for organizations to trim the cost of new systems.

The scenario does, however, point out the significant people issues involved in this kind of change. The huge change is not only in the software but also in the staffing needs that organizations will have in this situation. Gurus, like Todd, just won't be needed on an ongoing basis any more. They may be needed on the front-end design stage, but that will be it.

This shift has huge issues for organizations in a number of ways. As in the earlier case of Betty, Todd was bringing up arcane issues that seemed outside of the satisfactory technical reviews that were taking place. This should be a clue to management that resistance may be part of the picture. Todd may not be aware of his personal interest in redesigning the system, but it does appear that this is a wasted opportunity for the organization.

Suggestions to Overcome Resistance

• Selecting the right people

• A second set of eyes

• Get resistance out in the open

The challenge for management is to find a way that Todd's abilities can be used in a positive way, rather in the negative way that has emerged in this situation. If no answer can be found, it is probably better for Todd that he try to move on before his technical skills become out of date. Although his relationship with the CEO might seem to make him invulnerable to change, a better point of view would be to use that relationship to help him find a fit where his skills would be of use.

The Elephant in the Room

George was a vice president of benefits who saw his organization as excelling at providing specific internal services to their employees. He wanted a system that, as he described it, would be the "Cadillac of systems" to support those services. Having established himself as an internationally recognized expert in this area of internal services, he had convinced upper management to fund this effort.

Early on, an outside consultant was brought in by the IT department to help define the needs of this internal system. It was clear to the consultant that there were several commercial systems on the market that would easily support the needs of these internal systems. The IT department told the consultant to not bring up this possibility because it was important to George to build his own system and George was a VP. In fact, George saw the organization eventually selling his "Cadillac" system to other organizations.

Building such a system was more expensive than buying one on the market. No one in IT, however, ever brought up the idea of buying a commercial product rather than building one. While this system was being built, the organization's income decreased significantly in areas independent of the development effort. As a result, it was determined that it did not make sense to spend this much money on such a fancy internal system. The project was canceled after already spending many times more money than a commercial product would have cost.

Resistance Issues

- Not invented here
- Power of internal "expert"
- Our problems are special

Telling the truth about technology can be a politically painful event, especially when people in high places are the people who need the message. Many a manager has had to deal with a "pet project" of upper management.

Suggestions to Overcome Resistance

- Communicate at many levels
- Get resistance out in the open

This is a case when "managing up" would be a good idea. In this scenario, no one even raised the idea that commercially available software might work as well. Carefully planting the idea that this is possible could be done in many ways so that the VP could get the message clearly. The VP's need to have a special product might also have been addressed on another project.

Worksheet for Change Issues and Responses

The resistance scenarios provide some examples of change issues and the possible responses. Of course, you may have other change issues in your organization that may benefit from different sorts of responses. Figure 8.4 provides a worksheet you can use to think about restraining forces you may have added to Figure 8.3 and possible responses you could consider.

Consolidated Analysis for Adopting a Service-Oriented Architecture

Figure 8.5 consolidates the driving and restraining technical forces from Figure 8.2 and the driving and restraining forces related to change from Figure 8.3. The restraining technical forces that will fade away over time (the ones shown in gray in Figure 8.2) have been removed from this figure. Figure 8.5 shows that using Web Services reduces the technical issues restraining the

Change issues

Change issues	Selecting the right people	A second set of eyes	Really listen	Communicate on many levels	Seek appropriate avenues to involve people	Get resistance out in the open
Lack of training/understanding						
Power of internal "expert"						
Inertia – why change?						
Feeling that jobs may be threatened						
Not invented here						
Our problems are special						

Responses

FIGURE 8.4 Change issues and responses worksheet.

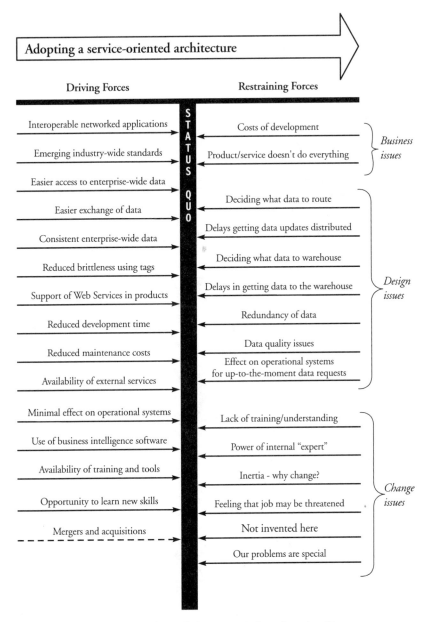

FIGURE 8.5 Force field analysis of adopting a service-oriented architecture.

adoption of service-oriented architectures and leaves us with business, design, and change issues. Business and design issues will always be with us. Change issues will form the biggest obstacles to the adoption of service-oriented architectures.

Summary

Web Services are rapidly removing many of the technical restraining forces related to adopting a service-oriented architecture. At the same time, Web Services are adding technical driving forces toward adoption. As a result, the primary restraining forces within organizations for adoption of service-oriented architectures have to do with business issues, design issues, and resistance to change. Business and design issues are part of developing any architecture. Change issues, however, could trip up the adoption of a service-oriented architecture. Ways to identify and overcome resistance were covered in this chapter along with scenarios of various forms of resistance. The next chapter will expand on dealing with resistance by providing some tips for managing change issues.

CHAPTER 9

Tips for Managing Change Issues during Development

Developing information systems is a complex activity with many tasks to accomplish, usually with many restraints as well. As with any human endeavor, there are easy ways and hard ways to do anything. This chapter will provide tips on how to make development easier.

The tips in this chapter come from my development and consulting experiences since the mid-1980s. They are not intended to be comprehensive. Nevertheless, these tips just might help you with managing change issues during development.

➤ According to a study by the Standish Group, nearly a quarter of commercial software projects were canceled outright in 2000. Poor planning and management were cited as the primary reasons. The canceled projects cost firms $67 billion. Projects not canceled had overruns of $21 billion. Software maintenance related to repairing defects averages 80 percent of IT budgets.[1]

Design as Little as Possible

If you haven't experienced "analysis paralysis," you are a rare member of our profession. The design of a system can sometimes seem as if it will go on forever. Based on my experience, both internally and externally to organizations, the best tip I can give you is to design as little as possible. It may sound counterintuitive, but most of the successful projects I have seen are based on as little design as possible. How do you do this? Two suggestions are to buy a

---

1. The Standish Group, CHAOS Report, 2000.

system or buy a model. Either of these tips will narrow the amount of design that you must do.

Buy a System

When you buy a software package, you are essentially leveraging a system that you can plug into your overall architecture. Doing this will limit the design work needed. You can focus on the connections in your architecture and the unique parts of it that you must design for yourself.

When considering packages, be sure they can participate in a service-oriented architecture. As Web Services are adopted throughout our industry, it will also become increasingly possible to buy "plug-compatible" software components that you can assemble into a service-oriented architecture.

The change issues you will likely encounter are:

- **Feeling that jobs may be threatened.** Yes, in many cases they might be. You will need to plan for this eventuality.

- **Our problems are special.** Yes, there are probably some special problems, but should they be driving your development? In the rare case, I have seen this to be true. In most organizations, however, there aren't special problems and if you look at the problems in a different way, it is possible to see how software packages can address those problems.

Buy a Model

If there are good reasons to not buy a software package, you don't need to start with a clean sheet of paper. There are data models available for purchase that are applicable to most segments of industry. Often these are referred to as *universal data models*. Universal data models can work with both data warehouses/master databases (see pages 50 and 133) or with middle-tier databases (see page 175).

I cannot begin to tell you how many times I have seen people struggling to model the same data repeatedly. Frankly, how many different ways are there to model customers, employees, addresses, products, and so on? Yes, there are variations among companies. But, if you look at the universal data models, many of those variations are handled in elegant ways. In fact, usually very experienced data modelers develop the universal data models—often these folks are more experienced than any modelers you might find in your organization. Months—yes, months—of modeling efforts in an organization fall short of almost any universal model you might be able to purchase. And, if you need to add something to these models, it is usually a minor addition requiring minor modeling.

The change issues you will likely encounter are:

- **Lack of training/understanding.** The plain fact of the matter is that when confronted with a universal data model, many people don't see how it will work. Often, it is because they are stuck in their paradigm of how the system should work, based on what they've experienced. They are simply trying to "map" the current system or their understanding of the current system, however limited it may be, to the universal data model. This is a stretch for many people. The best way to handle this is to bring in the developer of the universal model to explain how it will handle the needs of your systems.

- **Power of the internal "expert."** Oh my goodness—bringing in a universal model can really threaten this person. Telling anyone that a purchased product will be better than something that this person, an expert after all, could put together, is a very difficult sell. You will need to plan for significant resistance here. The previous chapter provides some suggestions.

- **Not invented here.** It is really tough to realize that other people have actually addressed many of your modeling issues. Even worse is the possibility that someone else may have done a better job.

- **Our problems are special.** This might be true around the fringes of a universal data model. In a rare case, it might be true for the model itself. But, be sure to thoroughly search for universal data models before accepting your problems are truly special.

Write as Little Code as Possible

This sounds a bit facile, but it is true. Time and again, I see people writing more code than necessary. Couple this with the fact that on average, professional coders make 100 to 150 errors per thousand lines of code,[2] you want to write as little code as possible just to minimize the errors.

Of course, buying systems and buying models will reduce the code you write. You should consider those options first. Again, as Web Services are adopted throughout our industry, it will become increasingly possible to buy "plug-compatible" software components that you can assemble into a service-oriented architecture.

If you have to write code, take a serious look at the systems you have. How many times have you written the same code to validate a customer account? I know some managers who have been able to identify the relatively

---

2. Multiyear study of 13,000 programs conducted by Carnegie Mellon.

few procedures they have that have been written repeatedly. Factor those out. You might save as much as 50 percent on future development.

Reduce Project Scope

Some of the new development methodologies[3] are emphasizing reduced project scope and reduced project times. It is so tempting to create big projects. The manager has to come up with ways to minimize the scope of each project. Multiyear projects are unthinkable. Twelve-month projects should be looked at skeptically. The challenge to the manager is to create projects that can be completed in less than 12 months.

Related to reducing project scope is building a service-oriented architecture incrementally. Part III provides specific suggestions in this area.

Use a Methodology

In more than 10 years of consulting, I have only rarely encountered companies that are really using any software methodology. Sure, they may say they are, but in reality they are still "shooting from the hip" when developing software.

Any methodology is better than no methodology. Yes, you can argue as to one being better than another, but the plain fact of the matter is that if you truly follow any methodology, you are going to be much better off than just paying lip service to the methodology or simply not using one.[4]

To really take advantage of a methodology, invest in a tool that supports the methodology. Paper systems or drawing tools that are not integrated with the methodology are not very helpful. It also allows people to slide by on the rigors of any particular methodology.

Use a Second Set of Eyes

Many methodologies involve having at least one other person look at any particular piece of work. Using a "second set of eyes" is critical. The trick, how-

---

3. Various agile programming or extreme programming techniques are currently being promoted. They are part of a long line of efforts to improve the quality of programming at the same time reducing development time and cost.

4. One person who reviewed this manuscript commented that methodologies could be used as another form of resistance. He described how entrenched experts in an organization can use methodologies as a covert means to ensure a project gets nowhere because of "the demands of the methodology." A variant of this would be using methodologies inappropriate for an organization, thereby slowing development. I guess you need to be ever vigilant to resistance issues.

ever, is really using a second set of eyes. Have you been in a big room for code reviews where the programmer describes what is going on in the program and everyone more or less nods their way through the review? How good is that really? Methodologies that require someone other than the author to describe what is going on in an architecture, design, program, and so on, are much more effective. It requires that person's second set of eyes to really look and that second mind to really understand.

Use Small Teams

For years, I have been recommending that people think of the communication issues in software development to be much like a dinner party. When you have a dinner party of seven or less, it is usually possible to have one conversation. As soon as you have eight or more people at the table, the dinner party breaks into two conversations and no one hears everything that was said.

This is often what happens in software development. Communication is critical. Use a small team. Put them together in a big room. Let them focus on development of their project; that means that the project is the only thing they are doing.

Summary

As stated at the outset of this chapter, these tips came from my development and consulting experience since the mid-1980s. They are meant to improve your chances of being successful with your development efforts.

The next part of the book provides some suggestions for reducing the scope of projects related to creating service-oriented architectures. It also provides specific suggestions for buying systems and reducing the code written.

Creating Service-Oriented Architectures

In Part III, the focus shifts to the creation of service-oriented architectures. Referencing the stages of adoption for Web Services and service-oriented architectures, Chapter 10 illustrates possible architectures for each stage. In addition to technical issues, staffing and change issues are covered for each stage as well. Several basic architectural options for service-oriented architectures are introduced in Chapter 11. Using a middle-tier architecture is one of the options covered. Middle-tier in-memory caching options along with the issues surrounding a middle-tier application cache are reviewed in Chapter 12. This chapter also considers the advantages of middle-tier persistence options. Finally, in Chapter 13, C. R.'s business trip from Chapter 1 is revisited with the details about the Web Services and service-oriented architectures used in the story, as well as some of the architectural options used.

Before jumping into these architectures, note that they will work with either Java application servers or .NET. You will not see any references to either environment, and the generic "application server" will be used instead.

Thank you for your interest in Oracle Business Integration. Please find the enclosed book— *Web Services and Service-Oriented Architectures: The Savvy Manager's Guide.*

We hope you'll find this book useful and that you'll look to Oracle Business Integration, built on unique Oracle Grid Technology, to connect your systems and implement a complete service-oriented architecture strategy. You'll gain a single standardized solution for design, deployment, and management while delivering end-to-end process automation.

For more information about Oracle Business Integration, please call 1.800.533.3795.

040833 arch

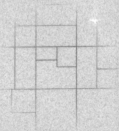

CHAPTER 10

Architectures at Each Stage of Adoption for Web Services

This chapter illustrates possible architectures to consider at each stage of adoption for Web Services and service-oriented architectures. In addition to technical issues, staffing and change issues are covered for each stage of adoption. The stages of adoption used in this chapter were first introduced in Chapter 7.

Architectures will be introduced at each stage of adoption. This is not intended to replace other methodologies. Rather, practical suggestions are provided that can be used with design methodologies.

Note that the length of time is not provided for each stage of adoption. The time each stage may take is entirely dependent on the organization, its needs, and its culture.

Stage 1. Experiment with Web Services

The best way to get started with Web Services is to start with small projects that have a high chance of success. Keeping the use of Web Services to something basic further enhances the chance of success. Choose a project that will be helpful, but not vital. Choose team members who like to play with possibilities. And be sure to communicate that the project is an experiment.

Use an External Service

Probably the most basic place to start is using an external service. They are many simple external services from which to choose. For example, you could get weather or stock information or track packages. More examples of relatively simple external services can be found at www.xmethods.net.

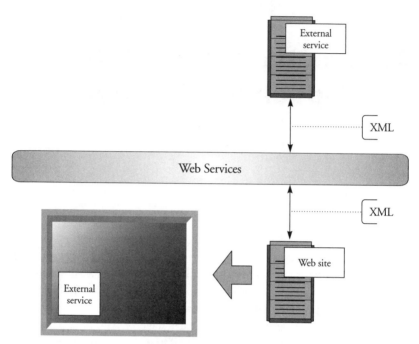

FIGURE 10.1 Using an external service.

Figure 10.1 illustrates using an external service. Such an experimental project would provide experience at using SOAP, possibly using Universal Description, Discovery, and Integration (UDDI) or other directories, and using Web Services Description Language (WSDL) and XML for sending and receiving messages.

Using an external service will help your organization try Web Services without a large outlay of time and money. It will give you an idea of how Web Services work and where you might want to try your hand at developing an internal service.

Develop an Internal Service

Developing an internal service allows your organization to get more deeply into development. There are two options for developing an internal service. The first is to develop an entirely new service that uses Web Services. For most companies, a second option of developing a service that uses some existing system would provide experience more in line with how Web Services will be used internally.

Figure 10.2 shows an internal portal accessing a mainframe or other internal system via Web Services. Examples of such access include obtaining customer contact information or internal employee telephone numbers.

This experiment requires the development of an adapter that transforms a SOAP message containing XML into an existing record format that can be accepted by the mainframe system. This project builds on the experience of using SOAP with an external service and adds complexity by developing an adapter. Of course, if your organization is more likely to buy all its adapters, this would be an opportunity to buy a commercially available adapter for an existing system and incorporate that adapter into this project. Nevertheless, even if your organization will most likely buy its adapters, building a simple adapter may be a good learning experience. Building an adapter will give your developers a deeper understanding of the functions of purchased adapters.

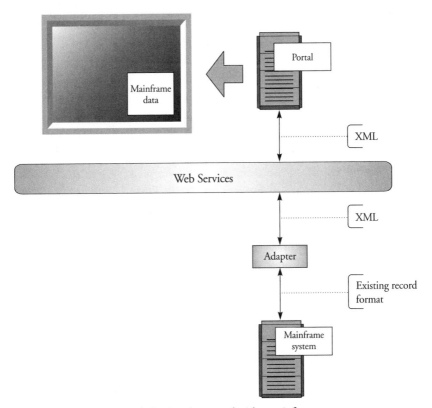

FIGURE 10.2 Using Web Services in a portal with a mainframe system.

Exchange Data between Existing Systems

If your organization is likely to use Web Services to exchange data between existing internal systems, then it would be appropriate to add an experimental project that does just that. Figure 10.3 illustrates this exchange of data between internal systems.

This project uses the experience from the last experimental project of building or using a commercially available adapter. In this project, however, two internal systems exchange data. For example, both systems A and B may allow users to enter customer address and contact information. If one system updates this customer information, the other system should also receive the update. Another example might be that system A has the master account for customer information and system B may request system A to validate that a customer identification number is correct.

Both systems A and B would need adapters. The development would require agreement on the semantics of the XML messages exchanged by the adapters. This would create the opportunity to investigate and possibly use the XML tags provided by standards efforts in your industry.

Develop a Simple Message Router

Many organizations are also likely to use a message router in a service-oriented architecture. The message router will need to check the XML message tag to see which systems might need to receive the data. Figure 10.4 shows the use of a message router.

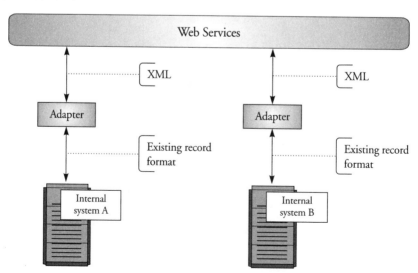

FIGURE 10.3 Using Web Services to exchange data between internal systems.

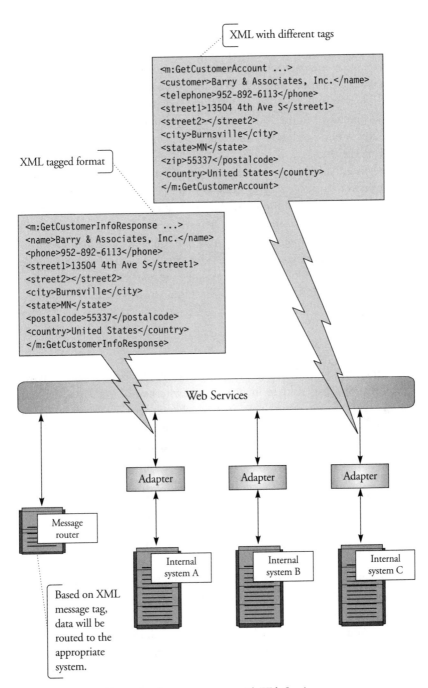

FIGURE 10.4 Using a simple message router with Web Services.

An example similar to the last experimental project would be where both systems A and B may allow users to enter customer address and contact information. All three systems in Figure 10.4, however, would need to receive this information. A message router would be set up to receive all the customer updates and then route the updates to the appropriate systems. It also might be possible that system C uses a commercial adapter that uses different XML tags. This is shown in the XML message fragments in Figure 10.4. The message router would need to be capable of converting the XML tags in addition to routing the message.

The intent of this experimental project is to gain appreciation of the issues related to message routing as well as experience in developing a message router. Even if your organization is likely to buy a commercial message router, it may be worthwhile to develop your own for this experiment. Much like writing your own adapters, building a simple router may be a good learning experience and building a router will give your developers a deeper understanding of the functions of purchased message routers. Nevertheless, don't overcomplicate this experimental project. Limit the project to routing one or two messages.

Staffing in Stage 1

It is important to pick the right people to do this experimentation. Frankly, in most situations, it is risky to involve people who have never expressed much interest in trying something new. Instead, choose people who like to experiment and take risks. For many organizations, it would be good to bring in someone from outside the organization who is familiar with Web Services and service-oriented architectures to mentor developers through the experiment. The mentor would be a "second set of eyes" during this experimentation stage and would be a great source of information. Keep the experimentation team small. A few people would be appropriate for most organizations.

Likely Change Issues in Stage 1

The most likely change issues you will encounter in this stage are:

- **Lack of training/understanding.** This is a rational concern. People are going to need training on Web Services and service-oriented architectures. You will need to find the appropriate training for those involved in the experimentation. Also, you need to be ready to dispel any misunderstandings concerning Web Services and service-oriented architectures.

- **Inertia—why change?** Be prepared to communicate on many levels and in many ways why you want this experimentation to occur. Be available for personal chats. Be prepared, as well, to really listen to concerns expressed.

Stage 2. Adapt Existing Systems to Use Web Services

Once you have some experience at using or building adapters, look for some places in your existing systems where using Web Services could save time and money in the short term. If your organization is like many others, you might have some type of common data that is replicated, which could be an opportunity. For example, you might have common customer data in multiple systems. These might be systems that were developed over time in separate departments or purchased software packages. They might be systems used by other organizations that your organization has acquired over time. In any case, the systems are likely to be different, have replicated data, and in some cases, inconsistent data. If there would be an advantage to creating more visibility of customers for such purposes as cross-selling among departments, creating new packages of products for specific customers, or simply reducing waste in misrouted or duplicated mail, this may by a worthwhile project to consider.

This section will provide step-by-step suggestions for using Web Services with a customer master file. The same steps should apply to other types of master data.

Create a Master Database

For some people, the very idea of creating any type of master file is discouraging. Many of us have had the experience of failed efforts to create master files (see page 162). Here are some tips:

- **Use an existing master file.** You might already have a master file that is part of packaged software your organization already owns. It might make sense to adopt that as the master file. If you do not have a master file in packaged software your organization owns, but are considering the purchase of packaged software, check to see if the software being considered includes a master file.

- **Buy a model.** This option is often overlooked. Many models can be purchased. Sometimes they are referred to as *universal data models* (see page 120). The plain fact is that, although every organization is unique in some way, most of the data is pretty standard. For example, there are practical and flexible models for keeping basic customer information such as addresses and other contact information. Often, these models are simply better than any one organization might build. Experienced modelers who have created models for many organizations usually are the people who design these models. If you buy a model, you should resist any efforts to extensively modify it. See the next tip.

- **Don't start a modeling project.** A modeling project opens your organization to any number of restraining forces including: our problems are special, power of an internal expert, and lack of training and understanding. The lack of training and understanding is significant. Data modeling appears deceptively simple until you get into it. Even if you are doing something as basic as a customer master, you can get yourself pretty knotted up in the options of data modeling. A modeling project also is an opportunity for people to add "bells and whistles" to a basic model. Starting a modeling project is essentially creating an environment for "analysis paralysis."

- **Start small.** Your master file does not need to be perfect. It simply needs to be useful or effective. Also, you can always add to your master file. So, if either a purchased master file or a purchased model have many fields you could populate, try to limit the master data to what might be most useful. Don't make the project any larger than it needs to be. You can always add more data to the master file later.

Figure 10.5 shows a customer master file at the left of the figure. At the right is an existing internal system, and existing applications are above the existing system. Those applications will remain unchanged in this process with one exception. Once customer master data from the existing system is

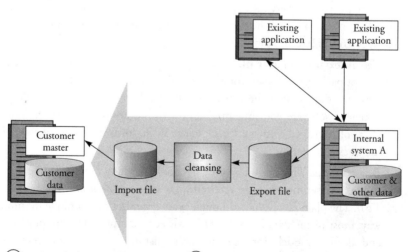

① Develop customer master   ② Populate master with clean data

FIGURE 10.5 Creating a customer master database.

moved to the master file, the existing applications may no longer update customer data. The reason for this will be explained in a little while.

Most organizations have multiple sources of customer data in their existing systems. This process will start with one existing system and then move on to others. To pick the first existing system, it might be one that is easy in some way. One way a system might be easy is that the data might be particularly accurate. Another way is that it might be easy to purchase or develop a Web Services adapter for a system. Read through the rest of the steps in this stage to see the requirements for this adapter.

Creating a master file is a good time to make sure the data you are using is the best possible. This process is often called data cleansing. Data cleansing can become a large project in itself, depending on the existing system and the number of existing systems that will be used for the customer master. You might consider purchasing an extract, transform, and load (see page 224) software product if you expect to use many existing systems that will require significant data cleansing.

At this point, some enterprise data warehouse (EDW) advocates are thinking that I have oversimplified what needs to be done. In a sense I have, but only because this master file is not an EDW. It is a small master file. It might grow into an EDW, but that is an entirely different project. At this point, the master file is meant to achieve a limited goal of consolidating a small amount of data—in this example, customer master data.

Connect Components to Web Services

Figure 10.6 shows the three components that are connected to Web Services. The first is the customer master database that has just been populated. The second is the message router. And the third is the existing system using a Web Services adapter. The experiments performed in the last stage should help you decide if you want to build or buy the message router and/or the adapter for your existing internal system.

Routing Master Database Updates

The experiments with a portal in stage one will help with this next step. Figure 10.7 shows adding an internal portal to this architecture. The portal will allow the user to read data from the internal existing system as well as the customer master. It will also allow updates to the customer master. It would be up to you to decide if this portal should be expanded to also allow updates to the existing internal system. Doing so would require adding additional message capabilities to the adapter for the existing internal system.

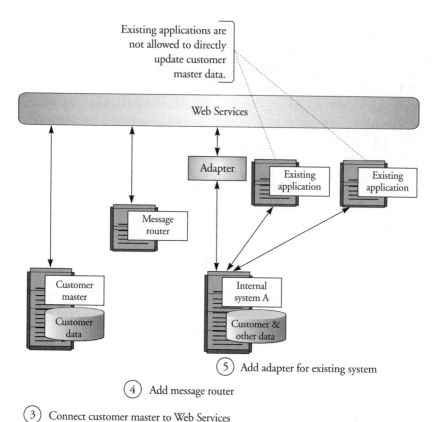

FIGURE 10.6   Connect components to Web Services.

The customer master system would perform two actions. First, it would attempt to update the customer data with the incoming data. If the update should fail for some reason, the appropriate error message is returned. If the update is successful, then the data used for the update is passed to the message router.

At this point in development, all customer master update capability in the existing applications needs to be disabled. Updates will come only from the customer master and through the message router. The existing system will have its customer data updated so that any existing applications needing to read that data from the existing system will continue to be able to do so. The only change is that these applications cannot update the customer master data that resides in the existing system.

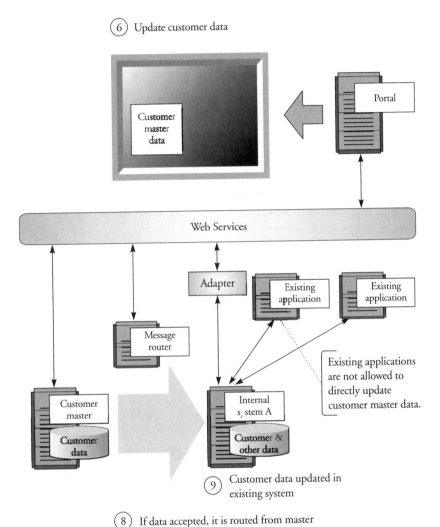

FIGURE 10.7 Routing master database updates.

By restricting updates to the customer master file, it is, in theory, possible to maintain the quality of data and consistency of customer master data. This is preserving the work done in the data cleansing stage.

Add Additional Systems

For each additional system, repeat the data cleansing and populating of customer master data. This might be an intensive process if you find inconsistencies among the data sources. Many of these inconsistencies will not be able to be resolved using programming. For example, if the same customer has two different addresses, it will be necessary for a person to determine if the addresses should be the same or if they represent two different locations of the same customer. Eventually, the architecture will look like Figure 10.8.

You might decide to have different portals for different departments that use different existing systems. This would allow tailoring of the portals to best meet the needs of the particular department.

Keep in mind that the master database could evolve into a data warehouse or a data mart. There is no requirement that an organization necessarily have a single data warehouse. A group of cooperating data marts might work just as well or better. A lot depends on the needs of the organization.

Message Router Options

Whether you build or buy a message router, there are options you should consider. These are shown in Figure 10.9.

The basic router included in the figures so far is in the lower left quadrant of Figure 10.9. It does not store messages and, should the machine it is running on fail, there is no secondary machine to take over to pass messages. Also, any messages in transit might be lost at the time of failure.

A more sophisticated type of message router is in the upper left quadrant. It stores messages. This means that a message sent to the message router can be viewed as being sent once the message router acknowledges receipt of the message. Since the messages are stored in some way, even if this message router should fail, all messages would eventually be sent on. Nevertheless, like the last router, there is no secondary machine to take over to pass messages should the primary machine fail. This means that if the message router is unavailable, no messages will be routed until it becomes available.

The two right quadrants represent highly available message routers. This is achieved though application server clusters or some other means of one application taking over for another. The lower right message router, however, runs the risk of a message getting lost at the moment one machine takes over for another. The upper right message router takes care of this issue by replicating the data. This, however, might slow down messaging. Nevertheless, if it is critical to your architecture that a message router always be available and never lose a message, you should consider a router as shown in the upper-right quadrant.

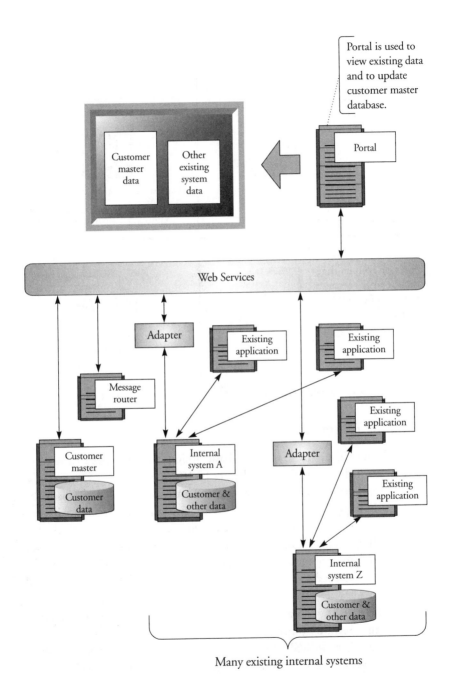

FIGURE 10.8 Using a portal and master database.

Not highly available | Highly available

Message routers that
store messages when
the messages cannot
be delivered

Database replication with application
server clusters or other means of one
application taking over for another

Message routers that
do not store messages
that cannot be
delivered

Application server clusters or other
means of one application taking over
for another

FIGURE 10.9   Message router options.

Database Options

Much like message routers, there are basic options for databases that need to
be considered. These are shown in Figure 10.10.

A basic database system is shown in the lower left quadrant. This is the
database shown in the figures so far. As with any database system, it will protect all data that is successfully updated even if the machine on which it is
running should fail. Nevertheless, this does not provide for a secondary
machine to take over should the primary machine fail. It also does not provide options for *load leveling* through using more than one machine. Load
leveling spreads activity or *load* across more than one machine.

The lower right quadrant shows a database system that uses *replication*. It
provides for a secondary machine to take over should the primary machine
fail. The data is replicated which means, depending on the type of replication, data will be available on the secondary machine should it need to take
over when the primary machine fails. (Replication options will be covered
later in this chapter.)

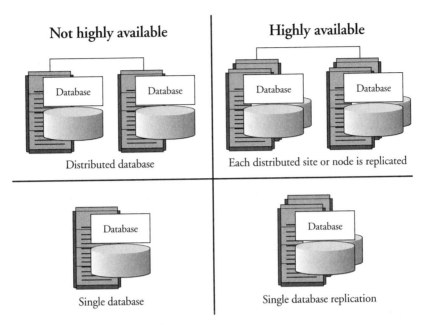

FIGURE 10.10 Database options.

The two upper quadrants show distributed databases, which is one way to load level access to the database. Databases can be distributed in the same location or in separate geographical locations. It is really a design issue. Not every system would need a distributed database, which can add complexity to a system. Nevertheless, there are architectures that can benefit from distributed databases.

The upper right quadrant shows a distributed database that also uses database replication at each node in the distributed database. This is one way to achieve both load leveling of database access and high availability through database replication.

Much like a message router, if the availability of the data in a master database is critical to your organization, then you should certainly consider database replication to make the database highly available. (By the way, the figure shows one replicated database in the right quadrant. Many products allow more than one replicated database if that should be needed for your architecture.)

Similarly, if the master database is pushed on access speed, then distributing the data among multiple machines is an option for load leveling this access.

Failover Options for Message Routers and Databases

The process of a secondary machine taking over for a primary machine is known as *failover*. Figure 10.11 shows three types of failover at the right. They apply to each of the message routers and databases at the left. The terminology for types of failover can vary. For this reason, each term is also defined at the right of the figure.

The first two forms of failover are acceptable for a service-oriented architecture, but the third form, application, is not in most cases. It would require applications that depend on a machine being available to detect the loss of the machine. This would mean, for example, that a message router would need to detect that the primary machine for a master database has failed and then route data to the secondary machine. Conversely, the machine handling the master database would need to detect the loss of the primary machine for the message router and route data to the secondary machine. This detection of machine loss among disparate components of a service-oriented architecture is too intertwined. It would be as if a videocassette recorder (VCR) would need to detect whether a television is running before the VCR would start a videotape.

- **Transparent copy:** the second machine takes over without the knowledge of the application

- **Transparent cluster:** in a clustered environment, if one node goes down, the remaining node(s) take over for the failed node without the knowledge of the application

- **Application:** the application needs to detect the loss of the master and switch to the second machine

FIGURE 10.11 Types of failover for both highly available message routers and databases.

Replication Options for Message Routers and Databases

Both message routers and databases could take advantage of replicated data. Four types of data replication are shown in Figure 10.12. The terminology for types of replication can vary. For this reason, each term is also defined at the right of the figure.

The only type of replication that will guarantee that no data is lost at time of failover is real-time replication. All the other forms can lose some data at failover time in one way or another.

Real-time replication, however, has a cost. It can double the time it takes to update the stored data in either a message router or a database. Nevertheless, if it is important to your architecture that no data be "lost" due to failover, then real-time replication is the only way to go.

Other options concerning replication have to do with how the primary and secondary sites can be used. Some systems allow only updates on the primary (sometimes called "master") site. The secondary (or "slave" or "replicated") site exists only to receive the secondary update. Other systems allow data to be updated on either the primary or secondary site. The first master/slave technique is simpler. The second technique may open up architectural opportunities. A lot depends on your organization's needs to determine which would be more useful.

Putting the Options Together

Figure 10.13 expands the architecture shown in Figure 10.8 to take advantage of some of the options for message routers and databases.

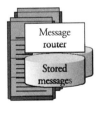

- **Real-time:** replication occurs as part of the same transaction

- **Store and forward:** replication occurs on a periodic basis

- **Time-based:** replication occurs at a set time of day

- **Event-based:** replication occurs at a specific event

FIGURE 10.12 Types of database replication for both message routers that store messages and databases.

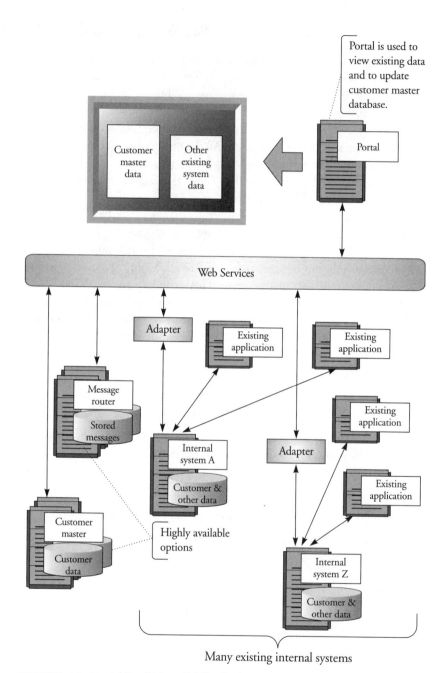

FIGURE 10.13 Adding high-availability for the customer master and message router.

The customer master in this figure is a replicated database that uses real-time replication, which increases the likelihood that it will be available at any point in time. The message router in this figure stores messages and also uses real-time replication. A receipt returned by the message router indicates that the message router guarantees delivery as long as the final destination service is available. A receipt would only be sent once the message was successfully stored and therefore, replicated in the message router.

For many organizations, having highly available master databases and message routers will be sufficient because they may be the only single points of failure that the rest of the architecture uses. If a particular service should fail, for example, the users of that service would be affected, but not all services, as could be the case if either master database or the message router should be unavailable.

In summary, highly available master databases and message routers:

- Reduce the risk of any one internal system not being able to complete processing that is dependent on data from another system.

- Require using fewer adapters since each internal system needs only to have an adapter that works with the message router.

- Reduce the possible negative impact of requests for data that are outside the normal processing of the internal system.

Staffing in Stage 2

If you look back to Figure 8.1, you will see that costs start to increase significantly in stage 2. This is because more people are getting involved. You should have at least one, perhaps two or three people who have a reasonable understanding of Web Services. They can form the core of this team along with a few new people. The entire team, however, should be under seven people. (See the discussion on page 123.) This is also a good time to establish the methodology that will be used going forward.

Likely Change Issues in Stage 2

The most likely change issues you will encounter in this stage are:

- **Lack of training/understanding.** This is still a rational concern. The new people will likely need training. Don't assume that the people who have been doing the experimentation are the right ones to do the training. It would be best to have the training done professionally so that any bad habits that may have crept in aren't passed along. Also, be ready to dispel any misunderstandings concerning Web Services and service-oriented architectures. This will likely require communication in many ways on many levels, including upper management.

- **Power of the internal "expert."** Be careful that an internal expert does not sink the project in this stage. It is important that you select the right people and plan for a second set of eyes for each person involved. This may help counter the internal expert if he or she is on the team.

- **Our problems are special.** This will show up if you buy a model. It will be important to get this resistance out in the open as soon as possible so that you can deal with it. Recall the "But It's So Complicated!" scenario on page 108. It could happen to you.

Stage 3. Remove Intersystem Dependencies

At this point, the architecture is starting to position your organization for more flexibility. In a real sense, it is moving towards the plug-compatibility mentioned in relation to the earlier examples of AV systems.

Positioning for Flexibility

In the previous stage, you probably started removing some intersystem dependencies. For example:

1. The portals separate the user interfaces from the underlying system. They also provide a familiar browser type interface for users. In theory, it would be possible to replace underlying systems with minimal impact on the portal.

2. Factoring out common data such the customer data in this example may reduce intersystem dependencies and then make it easier to replace one system with another. Figure 10.14 shows one such possible situation where the only common data shared by multiple systems is customer contact data. When this shared database system was purchased or developed, it may have been ideal to have the shared database. But just like buying monolithic AV systems, you may sacrifice something for that compatibility. Over time, it may become desirable to replace one or more of these systems with a more advanced version—perhaps from a different vendor—that does not use the common database structure. If each of the applications can update as well as read the customer data, then it is possible to selectively replace any of these applications since each can be viewed as a separate system. (This criterion will be explained in the next section on design considerations.) Moving customer contact data to a customer master database could do this. Of course, if more data in the shared

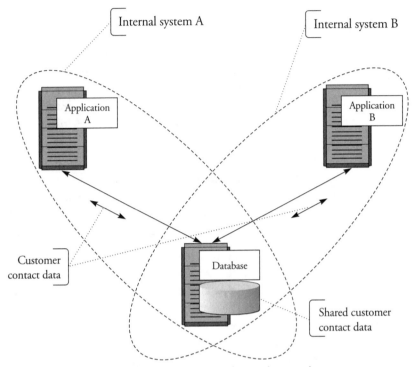

FIGURE 10.14 Shared database architecture that can be viewed as separate systems.

database is used by more than one of the systems, then the systems cannot be replaced. Nevertheless, that shared data might be the next candidate data to add to the master file in order that you can move your organization in the direction of plug-compatible software.

3. The master database and the router make it easier to add or replace software. Now a system or service added to this architecture needs:

   - A Web Services adapter that allows master data to be updated in its system—should it need the master data.

   - A Web Services adapter in order that other applications can obtain data. This would include any portals.

   - Of course, the router would also need to be updated in order to provide the appropriate data in a Web Services message that is "understandable" to the new system or service.

   - The master database and router are also replaceable since each has a set of Web Services interfaces.

Design Considerations

There are two overriding design considerations for intersystem dependencies:

1. **Factor out shared data.** Shared data might represent an opportunity to reduce intersystem dependencies. "Factoring out," does not mean removing data from the existing systems. It means moving the control of that data from the existing system to a master database, but continuing to update the data in the existing system using a router as described in the last stage of adoption.

2. **Each service is responsible for its own state.** This means that a service maintains its own data. This data could come from a master database through Web Services or it could come from existing applications. No data is updated on the side. If you want services to be plug-compatible, all messages and updates must come through the "front door," so to speak.

Figure 10.15 provides a variant of a shared database system. Application A is responsible for updating customer contact information among its other functions. Application B reads this customer contact data, but does not update it. Because Application B is dependent on Application A to update customer data, it is difficult to create a separate service out of Application B as it now stands because of this intersystem dependency. Application B does not maintain its own state because Application A updates the customer contact data.

When faced with a situation like that of Figure 10.15, you have two choices:

1. Factor out the customer data and plan to eventually replace both Applications A and B at the same time. This, however, would only make sense if at least one other system also uses customer data.

2. Modify Application B so that it is responsible for maintaining its own state by updating customer data. This disentangles the intersystem dependency.

So, primary activities in the stage are:

1. Determine applications that maintain data redundantly.

2. Factor out the redundantly maintained data into master databases, connect to message routers, and connect the applications to Web Services adapters.

3. Determine applications that use the same data from a shared database.

4. Determine if these applications should be separate systems.

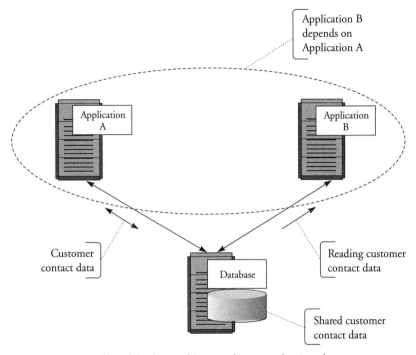

FIGURE 10.15 Shared database architecture that *cannot* be viewed as separate systems.

5. For those applications that could be separate systems, determine if they maintain their own state.

6. For those that do maintain their own state, factor out the data into master databases, connect to message routers, and connect the applications to Web Services adapters.

7. For those that do not maintain their own state, decide if multiple applications form one service. If so, and other applications redundantly maintain the same data, then factor out the redundantly maintained data into master databases, connect to message routers, and connect the applications to Web Services adapters.

Staffing in Stage 3

Much of this work should be able to be done with the team assembled for the last stage. By now, you should know whether it is a functioning team and whether it is able to move to this stage. If not, now is the time to change the team members.

Likely Change Issues in Stage 3

The most likely change issues you will encounter in this stage are:

- **Lack of training/understanding.** At this point, you must make sure that management has a good understanding of what is going on. It may look like you are "churning" systems for no reason if you don't communicate effectively what is going on. Be prepared to do this communication on many levels of the organization.

- **Power of the internal "expert."** If you had an internal "expert" on the team in the last stage, decide if it is an advantage or disadvantage to continue his or her involvement. You may want to keep the "expert" involved, but seek an appropriate avenue for his or her participation.

- **Inertia—why change?** This might occur at all levels of the organization. Be sure to get this concern out in the open early to avoid possible guerilla tactics. Once it is out in the open, you need to listen carefully to any concerns.

Stage 4. Establish an Internal Service-Oriented Architecture

By this time, your organization has the experience with Web Services that will allow you to establish a service-oriented architecture. Your experience will allow you to:

- Determine if you should use a data-centric, distributed-process architecture, or combine both approaches. These choices are discussed in detail in Chapter 11.

- Decide if a data warehouse, business intelligence software, or agents make sense for your architecture. These are also discussed in Chapter 11.

- Determine if your organization can take advantage of a middle-tier architecture. Middle-tier architectures are introduced in Chapter 11. Details on middle-tier in-memory caching and middle-tier persistence options are in Chapter 12.

"Fire" Should Come after "Ready, Aim"

I have waited until this point before suggesting that you establish an architecture, because the experiences of the first three stages are critical. An architecture based on experience is much more likely to succeed than one that is based on just reading a book or thinking about the technology. Without anchoring an architecture in what your organization really needs and your people are capable of accomplishing, then that architecture has a high likelihood of failing to achieve its goals. Stages 1 through 3 are "ready, aim" with this stage being "fire."

Design Considerations

There are three overriding design considerations when establishing a service-oriented architecture:

1. **Every service must be able to receive messages multiple times with no adverse effects.** For example, assume a service can receive updates to customer data. That service must be able to receive the same update more than once without affecting the data. The reason for this is that the sending service may, for various reasons, send data multiple times. This can happen when a system comes up after being down for a period of time. It may have some type of checkpoint that is taken after some multiple of messages go out. If the system goes down between checkpoints, some messages may need to be sent again to be sure they went out. It can also happen through mistakes in programming, multiple data requests, or simply unforeseen actions.

2. **High-volume, high-speed messages should be sent within a service and lower volume, lower speed messages should be sent between services.** This is one of those "relative" design considerations. Web Services, no matter what, are going to run significantly slower than processing within a service. Try to keep the high-volume, high-speed messages within a service. Figure 10.16 illustrates keeping high-volume, high-speed messages within a service.

3. **Balancing the conflict between operational access and ad hoc access.** It is common that the data structures that are best for ad hoc access are not the same as the data structures that are best for day-to-day operational access. Balancing this conflict is a challenge when creating an architecture. This conflict is quite apparent when providing both centralized master data and operational data as service to other departments over the Intranet or to other organizations over the Internet. The problem with ad hoc access is that you don't know when it will come or how long it will take. The access may require data that is consolidated from both master data and operational data. Yet, the users of the service expect responsiveness and that it be available all the time. Figure 10.17 illustrates this issue and provides a possible solution. A reasonable response is to establish a service-oriented architecture that takes advantage of the area shown as a cloud in Figure 10.17. This is referred to as the middle-tier and is introduced in Chapter 11 and expanded upon in Chapter 12.

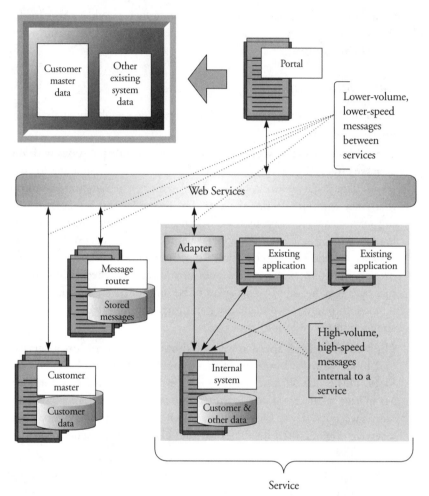

FIGURE 10.16 Keeping high-volume, high-speed messages within a service.

Staffing in Stage 4

By now, you should have an effective team of seven or fewer people who are very capable of taking on short-term projects. Your methodology should also be well established. Depending on your organization, you might need to establish one or more other teams of seven to deal with the work in this stage. The team members from the initial team could form the core of the new teams. This is a good time to have people in your organization self-select themselves into joining the additional teams. In this way, you are more likely to get the right people on the teams.

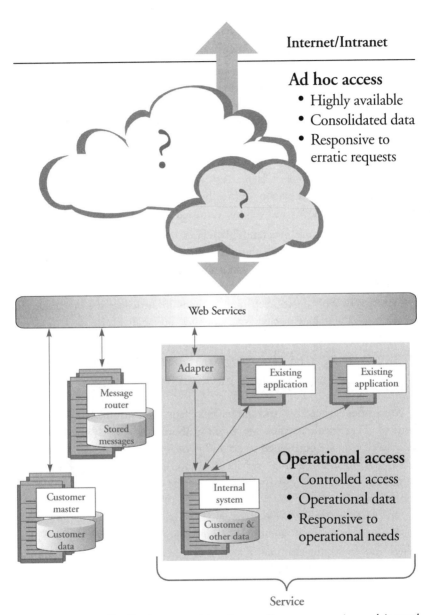

FIGURE 10.17 Conflict between ad hoc Internet/Intranet processing and internal processing.

Tips for Dealing with Change Issues in Stage 4

The most likely change issues you will encounter in this stage are:

- **Feeling that jobs may be threatened.** The s*** will really hit the fan in this stage. For many organizations, it will be obvious that the size of IT staff will be starting to go down and jobs may genuinely be threatened. Be prepared to communicate openly about this as soon as possible so that people have time to make decisions.

- **Not invented here.** You are likely to be considering packaged software or systems in this stage. It is very human to resist this. Be sure to get this resistance out in the open and really listen to concerns in order to make sure any legitimate concerns are addressed.

- **Our problems are special.** This relates to the feeling that jobs may be threatened. Be sure to get these concerns out in the open to see if there is any real concern the special issues are being overlooked. Chances are very likely that the problems are not special. Be prepared to communicate this effectively. Be sure to keep management informed as the word spreads through the grapevine that "special issues" are being overlooked.

Stage 5. Expand the Internal Service-Oriented Architecture to Include External Services

If you jumped ahead to read about this stage, you are likely to be disappointed. There really isn't too much to say about this stage. If you have done your work, you are positioned to expand your internal service-oriented architecture to include external services. I have been discussing this "plug-compatibility" throughout this book. At stage 5, you will be at the plug-compatibility stage.

In this stage, you will have the choice of weaving together services from other organizations with services your organization uniquely provides. This is where you could, for example, integrate an external CRM service much like what was described in the initial story about C. R.'s business trip.

Staffing in Stage 5

By now, you are sailing along. You might have several teams involved with weaving together Web Services. The team members' skills position you to be ready to change things quickly should there be a business need for changing some aspect of your service-oriented architecture in a hurry.

Likely Change Issues in Stage 5

The most likely change issues you will encounter in this stage are:

- **Not invented here.** As time goes on, more and more external services or services will be available so that you could purchase packaged software that could replace internal custom-built services. Be prepared to continue to address this resistance through proper communication of the advantages of these services to your organization.

- **Our problems are special.** This change issue is related to the last one. It is difficult for many people to realize that specific problems are not special. The opportunity lies in weaving together "not-so-special" services into a special architecture for your organization.

Summary

Chapter 7 introduced the stages of adoption for Web Services and service-oriented architectures. This chapter showed possible architectures to consider at each stage of adoption leading up to "plug-compatibility" of Web Services in the final stage. Tips on staffing and likely change issues for each stage were also provided for each stage of adoption.

There are some additional architectural options to consider with Web Services. The next chapter will discuss data-centric and distributed-process architectural options.

CHAPTER 11

Architectural Options

Several architectural options for service-oriented architectures are introduced in this chapter. All options are not covered, because that isn't possible. The very nature of Web Services will encourage the development of all sorts of interesting architectural options. So, by definition, there cannot be a complete list and any list that claims to be complete will be out-of-date tomorrow. Nevertheless, there are basic options that can be considered. These options serve as a foundation to which additional architectural options can be added. The two options that are covered are data-centric and distributed-process architectures.

Data-Centric Architecture

Up to this point, a data-centric architecture has been presented. It is "data-centric" because it is based on moving data to where the data might be needed. This is done with the message router and populating data in the various services.

The advantages of a data-centric architecture include:

- **Data quality is controlled.** There is one master copy of any data item, quality is controlled at that point, and every other data item is a duplicate of the master copy. The message router controls the design issue of redundancy of data.

- **Effect on operational systems is minimized.** These might be existing systems as well as new systems. The only impact that a data-centric architecture has occurs at the time of data update from the message router. This is to be expected and is most likely to have minimal effect.

- **Few components need to be highly available.** Generally, only the master database and message router need to be highly available in a data-centric architecture. Nevertheless, the specific needs of an organization may dictate that other systems and services are highly available.

The disadvantages of a data-centric architecture include:

- **Delays in getting data updates distributed.** Because data is routed, there may be delays. Sometimes up-to-the-moment updates are needed. A data-centric architecture does not provide that.

- **Deciding what data to route.** This is a design issue. It has to do with the factoring out of shared data introduced in the last chapter. The disadvantage is that the data needed to be routed needs to be determined relatively early in the design of a data-centric architecture. Of course, additional data can always be routed. Nevertheless, it is something that usually needs to be designed in early in the development of the architecture.

Distributed-Process Architecture

One alternative to a data-centric architecture is a distributed-process architecture. It is "distributed" because the processing occurs at multiple locations. These locations are either where the "owning" system has data or processes requests. This section will compare a distributed-process architecture to a data-centric architecture. It will also cover situations in which a distributed-process architecture should be considered.

Comparison to the Data-Centric Architecture

To compare the two approaches, let's look at a simple request to obtain all customer information. Figure 11.1 shows this request using a data-centric architecture. The data comes from one source: the customer master file. This is a highly available service. The request does not impact other internal systems.

Figure 11.2 shows the same request without a customer master file. The data would come from multiple locations. The requestor would deal with duplicates and possible inconsistencies in the data. Also, if any one of the internal systems were not available, then all the customer information would not be returned. Finally, requests like this are the bane of operation system administrators. Such requests can slow down operational systems and, more often than not, come at unplanned times.

To deal with the availability of data, each of the internal systems could be made highly available much like the customer master system in Figure 11.1. Highly available internal systems are shown in Figure 11.3. Each system

Data-centric architecture

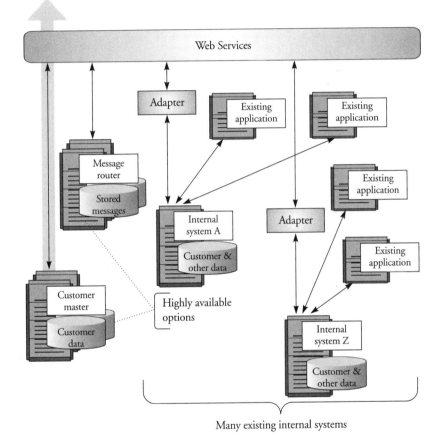

FIGURE 11.1 A response to a request for all customer data comes from one highly available source.

would need to be made highly available to match the availability of the customer master service.

Obviously, for this type of request, a distributed-process architecture would be considerably more costly to provide a highly available and complete response than a data-centric architecture.

Distributed-process architecture

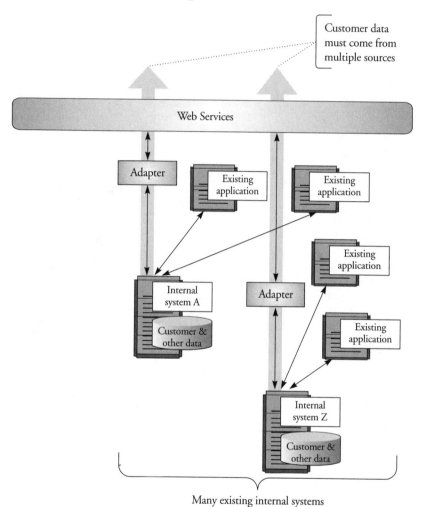

FIGURE 11.2 A response to a request for all customer data must come from multiple sources.

There are, however, very good reasons to consider a distributed-process architecture—particularly when you don't have to deal with data redundancy and consistency issues.

Distributed-process architecture

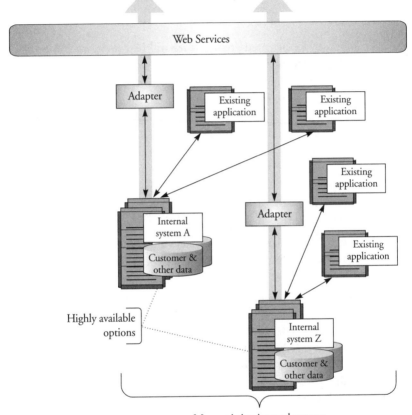

FIGURE 11.3 Adding high-availability to a distributed-process architecture.

When to Consider a Distributed-Process Architecture

The time to consider a distributed-process architecture is those situations in which it is critical to have up-to-the-moment processing or data. For example, in the story of C. R. in Chapter 1, it would be important to have up-to-the-moment information on car rentals along with airline and hotel reservations. In other applications, the very latest data on stock prices might be needed. In any case, if the data needs to be highly available, you will need to deploy the distributed-process architecture on highly available hardware and software.

Combining Data-Centric and Distributed-Process Architectures

In reality, most service-oriented architectures will be a combination of data-centric and distributed-process architectures. For example, when setting up C. R.'s trip, the travel agency service needed up-to-the-moment information for various reservations. To stay in business, services such as car rentals and airline reservations have to provide this up-to-the-moment data. The master database in C. R.'s organization, on the other hand, could have the arrival of updates delayed slightly with no impact on the organization.

Master Databases, Data Warehouses, Data Marts, and Business Intelligence Software

One benefit of a master database is that it has all sorts of useful information for your organization. These master databases could evolve into data warehouses and/or data marts. The design and maintenance of these are big issues—issues beyond the scope of this book. Nevertheless, data warehouses and/or data marts can play an important role in service-oriented architectures.

Master databases, data warehouses, and data marts open up the opportunity to use business intelligence (BI) software. BI software is another big issue that is beyond the scope of this book. There are, however, significant changes occurring with BI software in response to opportunities with Web Services. Some observations can be made.

BI software could be used for such things as determining patterns within your customer base and data mining. Because the opportunity also exists to create "clean" data in the master databases, data warehouses, and data marts, the value of this BI software to your organization may be quite high.

One option is to design databases that facilitate analysis by the appropriate types of BI packages. That may, however, conflict with the design of the database needed for day-to-day operations. Operational database access may be slow when a database is designed for analysis. Another type of conflict may occur when it is desirable to run BI analyses concurrent with heavy operation data loads. There would be a potential problem if the BI analyses slow down the operational data access.

There are several possible solutions to this conflict. This first would be to create separate data marts that are extracts from the master database. Using the BI packages with the data marts would mean that the analysis would not slow down the operational access. The disadvantage is that the data marts would not have the latest information. Organizational needs will dictate whether that is an important concern. Also, this does not address the potential conflict where operational database access may be slow when a database is designed for analysis.

A second solution would be to replicate and distribute the data in the master database. This is shown in Figure 11.4. The BI packages would work on the replicated database, thereby minimizing the impact of analysis on operational data access. It also allows the BI packages to receive the latest information since the replicated servers would be updated at the same time or nearly the same time as the master server.

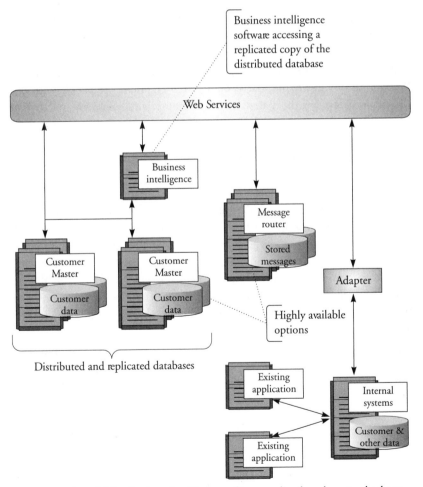

FIGURE 11.4 Adding business intelligence software to distributed master databases.

There is a third solution that involves using a middle-tier architecture. That will be described in more detail in the next chapter.

Agents

The term agent is a broad term to describe all sorts of systems that can enhance an architecture. In the story about C. R.'s business trip, automated agents played a major role in negotiating his travel plans and keeping C. R. up-to-date about customers he planned to visit. These agents communicated with each other using Web Services. The XML-tagged message formats aid in making the development of this communication easier.

Agents come in all forms and as time goes on, they will become more sophisticated. On a relatively simple side, there are agents that can help us shop online. As XML and Web Services are adopted, these shopping agents can become more intelligent. For example, without the XML-tagged formats, it is difficult for an agent to know if "blue" is the color of the sweater or a brand name. It is similar to the problem with using a search engine right now. If I look up my last name, Barry, on a search engine, I get people with that last name, people with "Barry" as a first name, and company and college names that include "Barry." An XML-tagged structure would allow a search engine to look for last names of "Barry." There would be a tag that identifies a last name. Similar identification will make it easier for sophisticated shopping agents to be constructed.

More sophisticated agents would be able to perform negotiations, monitor the status of systems, or monitor changes in the content of databases or other systems. For example, it is probably safe to assume that a master database is something that might be appropriate for an automated agent to monitor. Another agent might monitor an existing internal system. These agents could communicate with each other using Web Services or they could communicate with other systems internal or external to the organization using Web Services. Figure 11.5 illustrates adding agents to an internal service-oriented architecture.

Agent software is undergoing dramatic change right now. Simple agent software has been around for some time. More advanced agents are likely to appear as XML is adopted more widely. The reason is that agent software can take advantage of the semantics provided by the tagged structure of XML (see page 26).

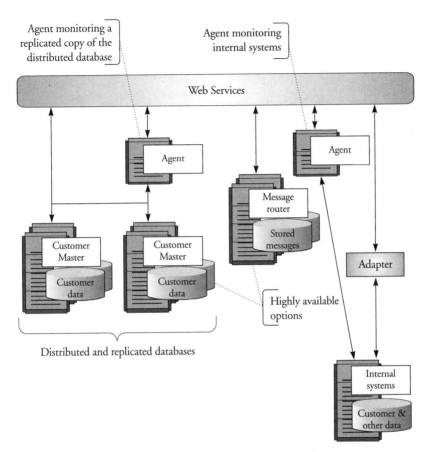

FIGURE 11.5 Adding agents to a master database and internal systems.

Summary

This chapter emphasized two basic architectural options: data-centric and process-centric architectures. In reality, nearly all service-oriented architectures will be a combination of both. Within these architectures, you will find master databases, business intelligence software, and agent software. The next chapter will show how these architectures can be enhanced with a middle-tier that is placed between the Internet or Intranet and internal systems and services.

CHAPTER 12

Middle-Tier Architecture

A middle-tier architecture is a common way to build Web Services using existing systems and databases. The middle tier changes where integration can occur. Instead of directly integrating existing systems and databases, a new layer can be developed so that the integration occurs in the middle tier. This is where you often find the use of *business objects*. Business objects are a way of representing something in the business domain, including various attributes, behavior, relationships, and constraints. Moving integration to the middle tier and using business objects is another solution to the conflict between ad hoc or analysis and operational access mentioned in the last chapter.

A discussion of business objects is outside the scope of this book. We will, however, cover the basics for a middle-tier architecture that provide an infrastructure for business objects. The discussion includes some options and tips to consider with such an architecture. Middle-tier caching, persistence, and firewalls are covered in this chapter.

Basics for a Middle-Tier Architecture

Figure 12.1 illustrates the basics of a middle-tier architecture. The internal systems and services that we have covered so far are at the bottom of the figure. They make up the enterprise information system tier or *EIS tier*.

The *middle tier* is above the EIS tier. The middle tier has a Web server that connects to the Internet or Intranet. The connections may be to services via Web Services external to subgroups in the organization or external to the organization. The connections may be to other Internet resources as well.

An application server is below the Web server. Either a Java application server or a .NET server could be used. Any type of application server creates

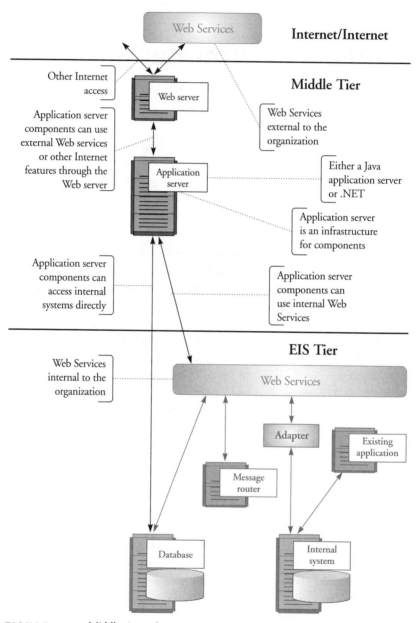

FIGURE 12.1 Middle-tier architecture.

an infrastructure for deploying applications that are usually called *components* (components is definitely an overused term). These components come in different varieties for Java application servers and .NET. The components are written in object programming languages such as Java, C#, C++, and others.

Components used in applications servers in the middle tier are a common way to realize the high-level abstractions of business processes and workflows that were discussed on page 78. Essentially the middle tier provides the opportunity to view both internal systems and services and external services in a different way that might be more consistent with the abstract models used in architecture frameworks.

An application server can have:

- **Access to external Web Services.** This could be virtually anything. In the story of C. R.'s business trip, it could be travel agent services.

- **Access to other Internet resources.** This also could be most anything: weather reports, currency converters, news feeds, and so on.

- **Access to internal Web Services.** An example of an internal Web Service might be the validation of an account based on data input over the Internet/Intranet and data stored in the EIS-tier database.

- **Access directly to internal system directly, bypassing Web Services.** Direct access to the EIS-tier database might be an example of this access.

Options with a middle-tier architecture include:

1. Middle-tier in-memory caching options
2. Middle-tier persistence options

Caching in the Middle Tier

Caching is the retention of data, usually in an application or application server, to minimize network traffic flow and/or disk access. Data from the EIS-tier database is cached in the application server. Caching in application servers is an important aspect of any service-oriented architecture. The application server, with its cache, generally resides in the middle tier of an architecture as shown in Figure 12.2. The cache resides in memory on the application server and retains data from the database in the EIS or bottom tier. The application server usually has a direct connection to the database in the EIS tier. Such a direct connection is made for performance reasons.

There are several ways that a cache could be populated:

1. **On an as-needed basis.** An *instance* moves into cache only when a program requests to read the values of the instance. (An instance could be a record, a row in a relational table, an object, or a portion of an XML document.)

2. **Fully populated at start time.** All instances needed in the cache are populated when the system starts up.

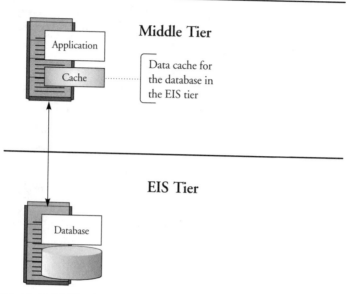

Internet/Intranet

FIGURE 12.2 Middle-tier in-memory data caching.

3. **A combination of the first two.** An example is populating the cache with the most likely instances that are needed and then moving additional instances into cache when a program requests to read the values of the instance.

Figure 12.3 shows various options for implementing in-memory caching. In the lower-left quadrant is a simple caching mechanism. There is one copy of the cache and should the machine on which the cache resides fail, the data that was cached becomes unavailable. Any data updates that were cached but not written to the database would be lost. Also, there is no opportunity for load leveling the activity against the cache since only one machine has the cache. Load leveling is important if the cache is accessed heavily.

In the upper left quadrant of Figure 12.3, cache replication is added. This allows for duplicate copies of the cache to exist on separate machines. This allows for load leveling of accesses to the cache. Updates to either copy of the cache are automatically replicated with the other copy. Although this option improves availability, it is not highly available. If the machine running the application server at the left should fail, then the connection to the database has failed. Updates to the database then cannot be made. Nevertheless, reading of data already cached could continue and will be adequate only if the

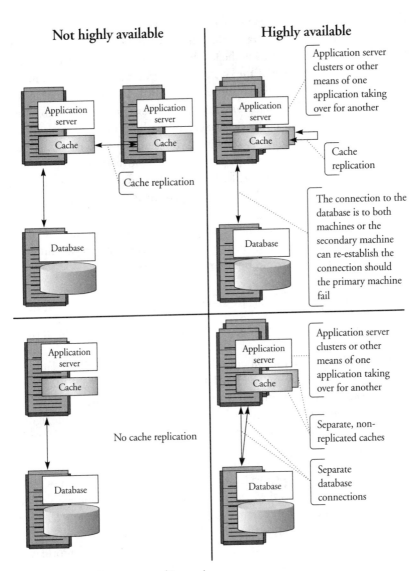

FIGURE 12.3 In-memory caching options.

entire database is cached in memory. If only a portion of the database is cached at any one time, it is easy to imagine a request not being able to be filled if the primary connection to the database is unavailable.

The right two quadrants of Figure 12.3 show options for making in-memory caching highly available. Both use application server clusters or some other means of one application server taking over for another. In the lower-right quadrant, the in-memory caches are not replicated. This means that should the primary machine fail, the secondary machine won't have an exact copy of the cache that was in the primary machine. A data update in the primary in-memory cache could be lost because the secondary machine does not have a duplicate copy of the cache. This is reduced by the option in the upper-right quadrant. Here the cache is replicated. If a data update in the cache was replicated before the primary machine fails, it is then possible that update could be picked up by the secondary machine and sent to the database. (This would be subject to some restrictions on transactions.) Nevertheless, the option in the upper-right quadrant provides for the highest availability of an in-memory cache. It would be appropriate to consider this option when in-memory caching for high performance and high availability is important.

The contents of a cache can be tables, objects, or XML. In any case, there are issues of keeping the contents of a cache synchronized with the underlying database. The next two sections cover these issues.

Caching Tables, Objects, or XML

Typically, the data cached at the application server level is either in the form of tables, objects (Java, C#, C++, or other object programming languages), or in the form of XML. Also, the source of the data is typically a relational database. Figure 12.4 shows tables in a relational database at the bottom of the figure. In the application server at the top of the figure is an in-memory cache. The options of caching tables, objects, or XML are shown at the top of the figure.

Mapping

When the cache contains either objects or XML, the transformation of tables into objects or XML is called *mapping*. Mapping is the technique used to make one or more rows in database tables appear as programming language objects or XML. There are many considerations to take into account when mapping between a database and cache. If you would like more information on these considerations, see www.service-architecture.com.

Cache Synchronization

An additional issue that needs to be considered is that a cache used by an application may not be tightly integrated with the underlying database. This problem is referred to as *cache synchronization*. It occurs after the data has been placed in an application cache. When only one application is using the data, cache synchronization is not a problem. As soon as a second application accesses the database, however, the problem can occur.

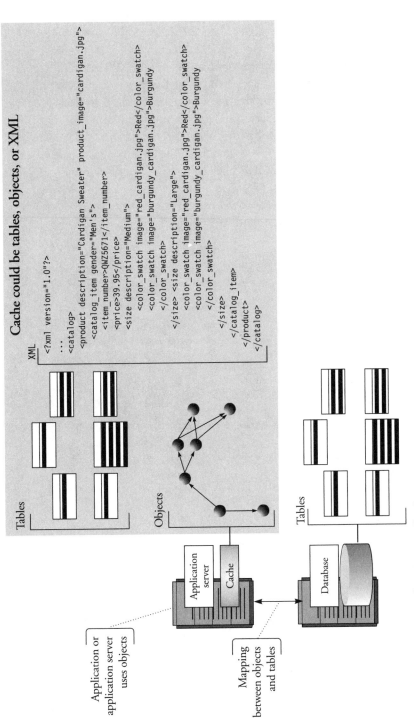

Cache could be tables, objects, or XML

XML

```xml
<?xml version="1.0"?>
...
<catalog>
  <product description="Cardigan Sweater" product_image="cardigan.jpg">
    <catalog_item gender="Men's">
      <item number>QWZ5671</item_number>
      <price>39.95</price>
      <size description="Medium">
        <color_swatch image="red_cardigan.jpg">Red</color_swatch>
        <color_swatch image="burgundy_cardigan.jpg">Burgundy
      </color_swatch>
    </size> <size description="Large">
        <color_swatch image="red_cardigan.jpg">Red</color_swatch>
        <color_swatch image="burgundy_cardigan.jpg">Burgundy
      </color_swatch>
    </size>
  </catalog_item>
</product>
</catalog>
```

Tables

Objects

Tables

Application
server

Cache

Database

Application or
application server
uses objects

Mapping
between objects
and tables

FIGURE 12.4 Data caching in an application server.

An example of the impact of a second application is shown Figure 12.5. In the example, a second application is accessing the same database server that is being used by an application that uses a cache with mapping. Application B can change the data being used by Application A. Cache A would need to be synchronized in some manner to obtain the changed data. How the cache is implemented will have a big impact on the problem. The data in the cache must be synchronized with the data in the database when a cache is used by an application that is separate from the underlying database server.

If both applications used a replicated cache as described in the section on caching that starts on page 171, then the cache for Application A would have been updated at the same time that the database was updated. This would eliminate the cache synchronization problem.

(1) Application A reads values of instance 1

(2) Application B reads values of instance 1

(3) Application B updates instance 1 and commits the update to the database

(4) Application A reads values of the cached instance 1 and has out-of-date data

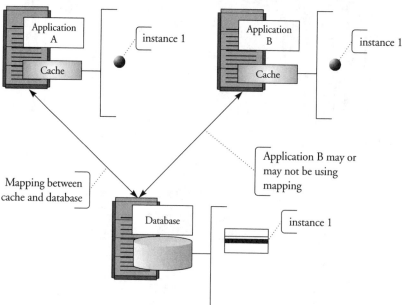

FIGURE 12.5 Cache synchronization issues for mapping.

Persistence in the Middle Tier

So far, we have seen how a cache can be used in the middle tier. It is also possible to add persistence to the middle tier. Adding persistence to the middle tier can make sense in situations that either have too much data to keep all the data in memory or situations where you need the protection of persistence to make sure no data would be lost before it can be written to the master database. It can also be a way to boost performance of services provided by an application server when it needs to access data.

The design of the middle-tier persistence should be such that it matches the needs of ad hoc data access. For example, in the case of our beginning story, C. R.'s organization may only keep the most recent contact information on only their active customers using middle-tier persistence.

Figure 12.6 illustrates middle-tier persistence. The middle-tier persistence is provided by the database just below the application server. There are two primary reasons to consider middle-tier persistence:

1. **Persistent cache in the middle tier.** The amount of data that needs to be cached for the database in the EIS tier is too much to keep in an in-memory cache. There might also be a need to protect the in-memory cache from machine failures.

2. **Consolidated data in the middle tier.** There may be data that is best consolidated in the middle tier.

Middle-tier persistence, however, will require additional development. This section will also provide suggestions of how to reduce that development cost and give you an idea what kind of performance gain could be achieved as a result of that additional development.

A persistent cache adds capabilities to the in-memory cache. These include:

- **Expanded caching.** An in-memory cache is limited by memory and the performance of virtual memory. A persistent cache offloads some of the in-memory requirements to disk.

- **Protected caching.** An in-memory cache will disappear if the machine on which it resides should fail. A persistent cache protects the contents of the in-memory cache.

- **Caching performance gain.** This depends on your architectural requirements, but it is generally possible to realize performance gains of 50 times or more using a persistent cache (see www.service-architecture.com).

All the examples in this section will assume that a database will be used in the middle tier to provide the persistent cache. A database manager ensures

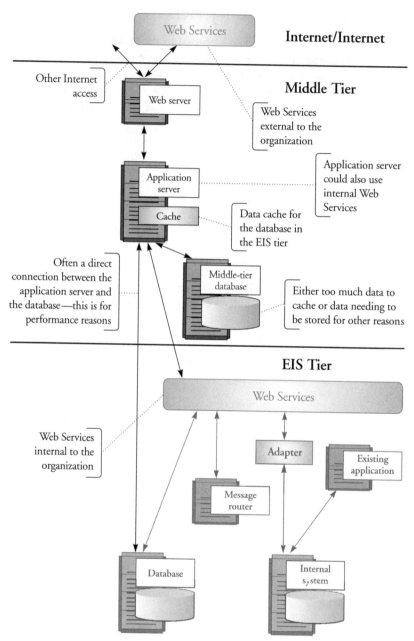

FIGURE 12.6 Middle-tier persistence.

that all transactions will be recorded properly and has recovery and backup capabilities, if needed.

Expanded Caching

Recall that there are several ways that a cache could be populated:

1. **On an as-needed basis.** An instance moves into cache only when a program requests to read the values of the instance.

2. **Fully populated at start time.** All instances needed in the cache are populated when the system starts up.

3. **A combination of the first two.** An example is populating the cache with the most likely instances that are needed and then moving an additional instance into cache when a program requests to read the values of the instance.

In any of these cases, the cache size simply could be too large to efficiently keep in memory. A middle-tier database could act as an expanded cache to offload some of the data cached in memory.

Using a middle-tier database as an expanded cache adds options when the underlying master database is updated. The updates could occur as they happen or at intervals, depending on the needs of the organization. For example, one option would be to populate the middle-tier database from the master database at the beginning of a business day. All updates could be kept in the middle-tier database. These updates could then be written to the master database at the end of the day or at intervals during the day. Of course, you would need to take any cache synchronization issues into account (see page 172).

Protected Caching

If all middle-tier cache updates are written to a middle-tier database, then the cached updates are not lost if the application server should fail. They can be recovered from the middle-tier database when the application server is restored. This, of course, would not be necessary if updates to the master record are made every time an update occurs. That, itself, can create a performance hit to the middle tier as will be discussed in the next section.

Caching Performance Gain

Tip The middle-tier database should use the same data model as the middle-tier application server cache to maximize performance.

If the middle-tier database uses the same data model as the middle-tier cache, there is a good chance that performance will be significantly better than if updates were written to the EIS-tier master database as they happened.

This performance gain is possible assuming:

- The EIS-tier database uses a traditional relational database structure. This is the most likely structure that the EIS-tier database will use.

- The application server uses a cache that matches the needs of the object program in the application server. This could be either an object or an XML cache.

- The middle-tier database uses the same data model as the cache.

Given these assumptions, the time it takes to write an update to the EIS-tier database will most likely take longer than writing to the middle-tier database would take. As the complexity of the model used by the object program increases, the greater the difference in the time it takes to write the update to the middle-tier database versus the EIS-tier database. This is because the mapping complexity also increases between the data model in the cache and the relational model in the EIS-tier database. The mapping simply takes time and costs performance (see www.service-architecture.com). As a result, an update to a middle-tier database can be significantly faster and allow the application to resume processing much sooner than if the update was to the EIS-tier database directly. Figure 12.7 shows the sequence of this processing.

This architecture can speed up the processing of the application server, often by 50 times or more (see www.service-architecture.com). Of course, you would have to take cache synchronization issues with this architecture into account (see page 172).

If you change the assumptions so that the application server uses a cache that matches the underlying EIS-tier database instead of one that matches the objects used by the application server, then this level of performance gain cannot be achieved. The reason is that the mapping between the cache and the objects used by the application server would need to occur each time an object is read from the cache or written to the cache by the application server. This mapping is in your application server program rather than below the cache. A middle-tier database still might make sense for other reasons, but it would not help improve caching performance in the middle tier.

Consolidated Data in Middle Tier

Consolidating data in the middle tier is another way to get a completely different view of systems and services. This opens up opportunities for the high-

Internet/Internet

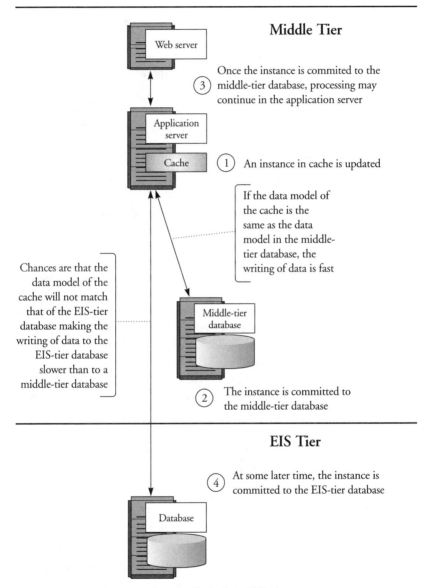

Middle Tier

Web server

③ Once the instance is commited to the middle-tier database, processing may continue in the application server

Application server

Cache   ① An instance in cache is updated

If the data model of the cache is the same as the data model in the middle-tier database, the writing of data is fast

Chances are that the data model of the cache will not match that of the EIS-tier database making the writing of data to the EIS-tier database slower than to a middle-tier database

Middle-tier database

② The instance is committed to the middle-tier database

EIS Tier

④ At some later time, the instance is committed to the EIS-tier database

Database

FIGURE 12.7 Using a persistent cache in the middle tier.

level abstractions of business processes and workflows that were discussed earlier in this chapter.

A few examples of middle-tier persistence could be online catalogs that take data from many internal sources, auction systems that need to provide high-speed access to the active auction items, or trading systems that need high-speed access to the items currently being traded or for only today's and yesterday's trades.

Figure 12.8 illustrates using a middle-tier database to consolidate data. The sources of data vary from manual input to internal systems data external to the organization. Generally, a characteristic of using consolidated data in the middle tier is an emphasis on performance. The impact this can have on the architecture is similar to using a middle-tier database for a persistent cache.

It is also important that the middle-tier database use a data model that is similar to the one used by the cache in the application server. Because the data used by an application server is either object data or XML, it makes sense that the cache and the database support either XML or the objects.

Middle-Tier Databases

There are many database options available for middle-tier persistence, because middle-tier databases essentially store temporary data. This is in contrast to EIS-tier databases that are often seen as databases of record, which are expected to last "forever." When you are considering a database product for an EIS-tier database, it is reasonable to choose a relational database product from a well-known, established company.

In contrast, middle-tier databases—because they are temporary—open up the possibilities of using technologies that might significantly improve performance and reduce development as well as maintenance costs.

There are many issues to consider in selecting a middle-tier database. A discussion of those issues goes beyond the scope of this book. More information on middle-tier persistence can be found at www.service-architecture.com.

Middle-Tier Firewall Options

One potential problem with service-oriented architecture is that the most common implementation of Web Services is to use SOAP. SOAP uses HTTP. This means that you would have HTTP going directly into your internal systems, which could be a significant security risk.

One way to solve this problem is to use an application server in front of a firewall as shown near the top of Figure 12.9. The potential for a "rogue

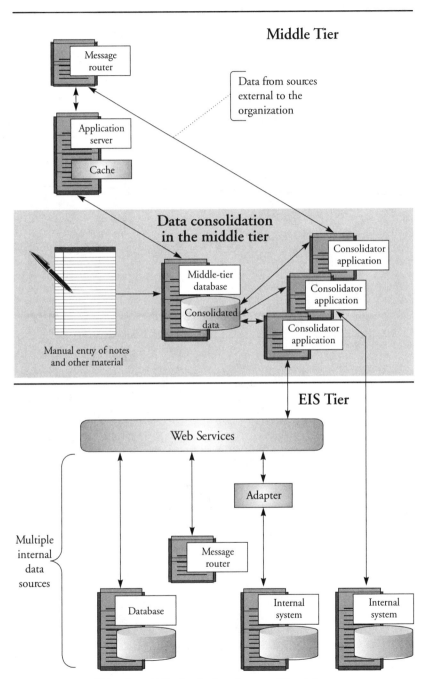

FIGURE 12.8 Using the middle-tier database for consolidated data.

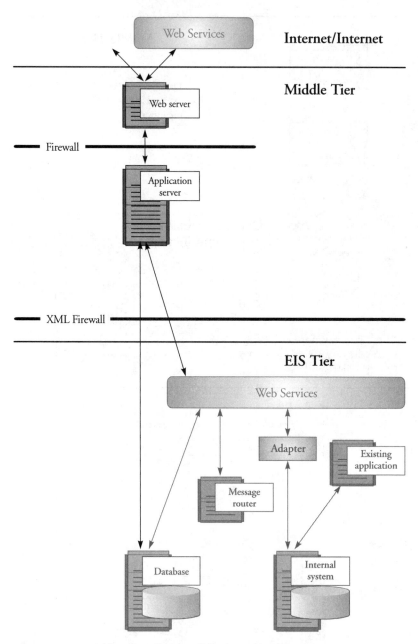

FIGURE 12.9 Adding firewalls to a middle-tier architecture.

message" moving through the application server is unlikely since the application server would need to create its own Web Services message to communicate with the internal Web Services or the internal database.

This architecture also adds an XML firewall above the internal Web Services to allow only defined messages from the application server to internal services in the EIS tier. Specialized XML firewalls offer the promise of protecting internal systems when using Web Services. Traditional firewalls offer protection at the packet level and do not examine the contents of messages. XML firewalls, on the other hand, examine the contents of messages. This includes the SOAP headers and the XML content. They are designed to permit authorized content to pass through the firewall.[1]

Summary

This chapter showed how much of what we covered in this book can be put together using a middle-tier architecture instead of directly integrating existing systems and databases. This chapter also showed that integration to the middle tier and using business objects is another solution to the conflict between ad hoc and operational access first raised in Chapter 10. Laced through this chapter are ways to make the middle-tier architecture highly available. Being highly available would be an important concern for many services offered using Web Services.

---

1. Also see the discussion of Web Services security and authorization on page 32.

CHAPTER 13

Revisiting the Business Trip in the Not-Too-Distant Future

Let's revisit C. R.'s business trip in Chapter 1 and look at the details for Web Services and service-oriented architectures along with some of the architectural options used in his story. As you read this chapter, page references to more on the topic are placed within parentheses.

The Business Trip

When C. R. sat down to set up his business trip, he used the portal Web site that appears near the center of Figure 13.1. He connected to the portal using a browser over Web Services. The portal had access to read internal information in C. R.'s organization as well as access to services on the Internet using Web Services (see pages 128–129). C. R. accessed the business intelligence (BI) software for selecting the customers to visit over his organization's Web Services (see page 162). The portal was designed to take the contact information from the messages returned by the BI software and pass the contact information along with other travel criteria C. R. provided to the Travel Agency service at the time C. R. selected the "Submit" button.

The messages from the portal are sent to the message router in the middle tier and then sent out to the Internet (see page 52). The portal also informed the internal Agent which customers C. R. would want to monitor (see page 164). The Travel Agency service took it from there, arranging the remainder of the trip and informing C. R. of any details that needed his attention. Eventually, his entire itinerary was sent to the portal. It is from this site that C. R. downloaded what he needed to his cellular telephone/palmtop.

When C. R. downloaded to his cellular telephone/palmtop, the connection to the portal used Web Services. At this time, C. R. also used his cellular

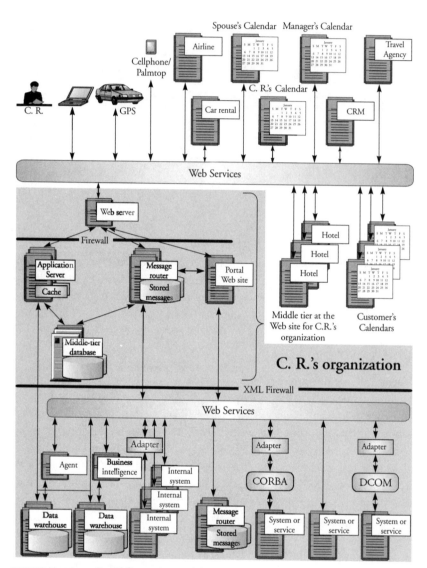

FIGURE 13.1 Detail for services and data interchange for C. R.'s business trip.

telephone/palmtop to command the portal to inform the internal Agent to start actively monitoring contact information on the list of customers he planned to visit. This also was a Web Services message. Monitoring by the internal Agent generated the instant text message informing C. R. that a significant problem had occurred. That message was sent through the middle-tier message router.

When C. R. was using the monitor and keyboard in his hotel room to get more information on a contact, he was using the middle-tier database at the left of Figure 13.1. This database contains all the recent customer contacts. It is a highly available database served by a highly available application server (see pages 167, 167). Note the two firewalls are used. The top one secures the data in the middle tier. The bottom XML firewall protects the internal systems and the internal Web Services (see page 182).

The information in the middle-tier database came from the data warehouse along with specific items from additional systems that used CORBA and DCOM connected to the internal Web Services using adapters (see page 45). The data warehouse at C. R.'s organization evolved from a relatively simple master database and is now distributed and replicated (see page 140). The agent works off one replicated node while the BI software uses another replicated node. This allows load leveling of the distributed primary nodes available for other processing. Also, to make sure all messages get transmitted, both message routers are also highly available and store messages for delayed transmission if the destination service is not available.

When, at intervals, C. R.'s palmtop transmits meeting contact information, it is in the form of Web Services messages that enter his organization through the middle tier at the left of Figure 13.1. First, it is stored in the middle-tier database. Then, the contact information is updated in the data warehouse. This is the same process used with contact information coming from the external Customer Relationship Management (CRM) service.

The scheduling changes, downloading of Global Positioning System (GPS) data, hotel reservations, and calendar updates were all handled by the Travel Agency service using Web Services without any impact on C. R.'s internal systems.

C. R.'s organization is at Stage 5 in its adoption of Web Services (see pages 89, 154). It weaved an effective service-oriented architecture from existing internal systems, a new data warehouse, a new middle-tier architecture, a portal for its "connected representatives," and a series of external services that interact using Web Services.

Summary

This chapter ties much of the technology of Web Services and service-oriented architectures back to the story of C. R.'s business trip at the beginning of this book. It illustrates what went on "behind the scenes" during C. R.'s business trip.

The next part of this book goes into more background on the technologies available with Web Services. It also has a chapter that serves as a quick reference guide for these technologies.

Compendium of Software Technology for Service-Oriented Architectures

Part IV provides more background on software technology and terminology that can be used in a service-oriented architecture. Chapter 14 provides additional details on specifications used in this book. Chapter 15 is a quick reference guide for software technology related to service-oriented architectures.

Additional Specification Details

This chapter provides additional details of some of the specifications discussed in this book. It starts out by providing a brief background on each of the organizations working on specifications related to Web Services. Then a matrix is provided that shows the various specifications and the organizations working on each specification. The latter part of the chapter provides details on important specifications:

- **Web Services specifications:** The most relevant specifications directly related to Web Services are included in this section.

- **XML specifications:** XML plays a significant role in Web Services. This section provides a brief background on many of the relevant XML specifications.

- **XML vocabularies:** Various industry groups have been developing the XML version of their respective vocabularies in order to take advantage of the XML messaging capability of Web Services. This section provides a sampling of those vocabularies.

Organizations Working on Specifications

This section provides a brief background on many of the important consortia and standards organizations working on specifications related to Web Services. At one time, software standards needed to be approved by the International Organization for Standardization (ISO) or the American National

Standards Institute (ANSI). The last decade or so, however, has seen the rise in importance of industry consortia developing standard specifications. The reasons for this vary, but industry consortia now play an important role in the creation of standards.

It may seem that with all the consortia and traditional standards bodies, the specification setting may become a competitive process. That does happen, but more often, you find organizations working together. Some examples include:

1. UDDI.org developed the initial release of Universal Description, Discovery, and Integration (UDDI) and then turned it over to Organization for the Advancement of Structured Information Standards (OASIS).

2. Blocks Extensible Exchange Protocol (BEEP) from The Internet Engineering Task Force (IETF) has a SOAP mapping. SOAP is from World Wide Web Consortium (W3C).

3. The adoption of W3C's SOAP in the electronic business using eXtensible Markup Language (ebXML) transport specification. RosettaNet also announced its adoption of the ebXML transport.

4. ebXML is sponsored by United Nations Centre for Trade Facilitation and Electronic Business (UN/CEFACT) and OASIS. OASIS has adopted specifications that resulted from this sponsorship.

5. Microsoft developed the C# object-programming language and submitted it to ECMA. C# is now an ECMA standard.

6. ContentGuard developed the eXtensible rights Markup Language (XrML) and contributed it as the base of a rights language in the Organization for the Advancement of Structured Information Standards (OASIS).

For links to the organizations included in this section or the latest information on relevant standards, go to www.service-architecture.com.

Business Process Management Initiative (BPMI.org)

The Business Process Management Initiative (BPMI.org) works on standards for the management of business processes that span multiple applications, corporate departments, and business partners.

electronic business using eXtensible Markup Language (ebXML)

ebXML, sponsored by UN/CEFACT and OASIS, is a modular suite of specifications that enables enterprises of any size and in any geographical location to conduct business over the Internet. Using ebXML, companies have a standard method to exchange business messages, conduct trading relationships, communicate data in common terms, and define and register business processes.

ECMA

ECMA is an international industry association dedicated to the standardization of information and communication systems. ECMA coordinates activities with the International Organization for Standardization (ISO) and the International Electrotechnical Commission (IEC).

The InterNational Committee for Information Technology Standards (INCITS)

The InterNational Committee for Information Technology Standards (INCITS) is the forum of choice for information technology developers, producers, and users for the creation and maintenance of formal de jure IT standards. INCITS is accredited by, and operates under rules approved by, the American National Standards Institute (ANSI).

The Internet Engineering Task Force (IETF)

The Internet Engineering Task Force (IETF) is an international community of network designers, operators, vendors, and researchers concerned with the evolution of the Internet architecture and the smooth operation of the Internet.

Java Community Process (JCP)

The Java Community Process (JCP) is an organization of international Java developers and licensees whose charter is to develop and revise Java technology specifications, reference implementations, and technology compatibility kits.

Organization for the Advancement of Structured Information Standards (OASIS)

OASIS is a not-for-profit, global consortium that drives the development, convergence, and adoption of e-business standards. Members themselves set the OASIS technical agenda, using a lightweight, open process expressly designed to promote industry consensus and unite disparate efforts. OASIS produces worldwide standards for security, Web Services, XML conformance, business transactions, electronic publishing, topic maps, and interoperability within and between marketplaces.

Object Management Group (OMG)

The Object Management Group (OMG) is a not-for-profit consortium that produces and maintains computer industry specifications for interoperable enterprise applications.

RosettaNet

RosettaNet is a self-funded, non-profit consortium of information technology, electronic components, and semiconductor manufacturing companies working to create and implement industry-wide, open e-business process standards. These standards form a common e-business language, aligning processes between supply chain partners on a global basis. RosettaNet is a subsidiary of the Uniform Code Council (UCC).

United Nations Centre for Trade Facilitation and Electronic Business (UN/CEFACT)

UN/CEFACT is the United Nations Centre for Trade Facilitation and Electronic Business. It is open to participation from Member States, intergovernmental organizations, and sectoral and industry associations recognized by the Economic and Social Council of the United Nations (ECOSOC). The Centre's objective is to be "inclusive" and it actively encourages organizations to contribute and help develop its recommendations and standards. Within the United Nations, UN/CEFACT is located in the Economic Commission for

Europe (UN/ECE), which is part of the United Nations network of regional commissions. These regional commissions report to the highest United Nations body in the area of economics, trade, and development: ECOSOC. The mission of UN/CEFACT is to improve the ability of business, trade, and administrative organizations, from developed, developing, and transitional economies, to exchange products and relevant services effectively—and so contribute to the growth of global commerce.

World Wide Web Consortium (W3C)

The World Wide Web Consortium (W3C) develops interoperable technologies (specifications, guidelines, software, and tools) and serves as a forum for information, commerce, communication, and collective understanding.

Matrix of Specifications and Organizations Working on Specifications

This matrix is meant to be an easy reference guide to see which organizations are working on specific specifications. The organizations are shown at the top. The specifications are categorized by the type of specification at the left. The specifications can be found in the next few sections or in the quick reference guide in Chapter 15.

	BPMI.org	ebXML (sponsored by OASIS and UN/CEFACT)	ECMA	IBM	IETF	INCITS	JCP	Microsoft	OASIS	OMG	RosettaNet	W3C	OpenWDDX.org	WSUI Working Group
Models and Meta-models														
Common Warehouse Meta-model (CWM)										X				
Meta-Object Facility (MOF)										X				
Model Driven Architecture (MDA)										X				
Unified Modeling Language (UML)										X				
Web Services Component Model									X					

	BPMI.org	ebXML (sponsored by OASIS and UN/CEFACT)	ECMA	IBM	IETF	INCITS	JCP	Microsoft	OASIS	OMG	RosettaNet	W3C	OpenWDDX.org	WSUI Working Group
User Interface														
Web Services for Interactive Applications (WSIA)									X					
Web Services Experience Language (WSXL)				X										
Web Services User Interface (WSUI)														X
Web Services for Remote Portals (WSRP)									X					

	BPMI.org	ebXML (sponsored by OASIS and UN/CEFACT)	ECMA	IBM	IETF	INCITS	JCP	Microsoft	OASIS	OMG	RosettaNet	W3C	OpenWDDX.org	WSUI Working Group
Workflow														
Web Services Flow Language (WSFL)				X										
Web Services Conversation Language (WSCL)												X		
XLANG								X						
Business Process Modeling Initiative (BPMI)	X													
Business Process Query Language (BPQL)	X													
Business Process Specification Schema (BPSS)		X												
Partner Interface Process (PIP)											X			

	BPMI.org	ebXML (sponsored by OASIS and UN/CEFACT)	ECMA	IBM	IETF	INCITS	JCP	Microsoft	OASIS	OMG	RosettaNet	W3C	OpenWDDX.org	WSUI Working Group
Repository														
Universal Description, Discovery, and Integration (UDDI)									X					
ebXML Registry		X												

	BPMI.org	ebXML (sponsored by OASIS and UN/CEFACT)	ECMA	IBM	IETF	INCITS	JCP	Microsoft	OASIS	OMG	RosettaNet	W3C	OpenWDDX.org	WSUI Working Group
Security and Authorization														
eXtensible Access Control Markup Language (XACML)									x					
eXtensible rights Markup Language (XrML)									x basis					
Security Assertion Markup Language (SAML)									x					
Service Provisioning Markup Language (SPML)									x					
XML Common Biometric Format (XCBF)									x					
XML Encryption												x		
XML Key Management Specification (XKMS)												x		
XML Signature												x		

Service	BPMI.org	ebXML (sponsored by OASIS and UN/CEFACT)	ECMA	IBM	IETF	INCITS	JCP	Microsoft	OASIS	OMG	RosettaNet	W3C	OpenWDDX.org	WSUI Working Group
Web Services Description Language (WSDL)												X		
Web Service Endpoint Language (WSEL)				X										
Partner Interface Process (PIP)											X			
Collaboration Protocol Profile/Agreement (CPP/A)		X												

	BPMI.org	ebXML (sponsored by OASIS and UN/CEFACT)	ECMA	IBM	IETF	INCITS	JCP	Microsoft	OASIS	OMG	RosettaNet	W3C	OpenWDDX.org	WSUI Working Group
Messaging														
SOAP												X		
Blocks Extensible Exchange Protocol (BEEP)					X									
XML Protocol (XMLP)												X		
Web Distributed Data Exchange (WDDX)													X	
RosettaNet Implementation Framework (RNIF)											X			
Message Service Specification (MSS)		X												

	BPMI.org	ebXML (sponsored by OASIS and UN/CEFACT)	ECMA	IBM	IETF	INCITS	JCP	Microsoft	OASIS	OMG	RosettaNet	W3C	OpenWDDX.org	WSUI Working Group
XML														
XML Schema												x		
RELAX NG									x					
eXtensible Stylesheet Language (XSL)												x		
XSL Formatting Objects (XSL-FO)												x		
XML Linking Language (Xlink)												x		
Java API for XML Parsing (JAXP)							x							
XML Namespaces												x		
XML Path Language (Xpath)												x		
XML Pointer Language (Xpointer)												x		
XSL Transformations (XSLT)												x		
Xquery												x		

	BPMI.org	ebXML (sponsored by OASIS and UN/CEFACT)	ECMA	IBM	IETF	INCITS	JCP	Microsoft	OASIS	OMG	RosettaNet	W3C	OpenWDDX.org	WSUI Working Group
Application Servers														
Enterprise Java Beans (EJB)							x							
J2EE							x							
.NET								x						
Object Programming Languages														
Java							x							
C++						x								
C#			x					x						

Web Services Specifications

This section contains the most relevant specifications related to Web Services. This is, by no means, the complete list. More specifications can be found in the quick reference guide in Chapter 15.

SOAP

SOAP provides the envelope for sending Web Services messages over the Internet/Internet. The envelope contains two parts:

1. An optional header providing information on authentication, encoding of data, or how a recipient of a SOAP message should process the message.

2. The body that contains the message. These messages can be defined using the WSDL specification.

SOAP commonly uses HTTP, but other protocols such as Simple Mail Transfer Protocol (SMTP) may be used. SOAP can be used to exchange complete documents or to call a remote procedure. (SOAP at one time stood for Simple Object Access Protocol. Now, the letters in the acronym have no particular meaning.[1]) Figure 14.1 provides a high-level view of the SOAP structure. For an example of how SOAP is used in Web Services, see page 22.

Blocks Extensible Exchange Protocol (BEEP)

BEEP from IETF defines a connection-oriented Internet protocol. A SOAP mapping for BEEP has been defined. SOAP messages inherit the additional qualities of service from BEEP for maintaining session context at the sender and the receiver. (SOAP itself does not maintain any context.) The context is used to create a connection that relates multiple messages as coming from the same source or intended for the same target. Security and transaction context can also be associated with a connection.

Universal Description, Discovery, and Integration (UDDI)

Universal Description, Discovery, and Integration (UDDI) provides the definition of a set of services supporting the description and discovery of (1) businesses, organizations, and other Web Services providers, (2) the Web Services they make available, and (3) the technical interfaces which may be used to

---

1. Starting with SOAP Version 1.2, SOAP no longer is an acronym standing for Simple Object Access Protocol. It is simply "SOAP."

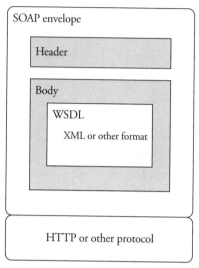

FIGURE 14.1   High-level view of the SOAP structure.

access those services. The idea is to "discover" organizations and the services that organizations offer, much like using a phone book or dialing information.

UDDI was first developed by UDDI.org and then transferred to OASIS. UDDI.org was comprised of more than 300 business and technology leaders working together to enable companies and applications to quickly, easily, and dynamically find, and use Web Services.

UDDI is based on a common set of industry standards, including HTTP, XML, XML Schema, and SOAP. It provides an infrastructure for a Web Services-based software environment for both publicly available services and services only exposed internally within an organization. The UDDI Business Registry system consists of three directories:

1. **UDDI white pages:** basic information such as a company name, address, and phone numbers, as well as other standard business identifiers like Dun & Bradstreet and tax numbers.

2. **UDDI yellow pages:** detailed business data, organized by relevant business classifications. The UDDI version of the yellow pages classifies businesses according to the newer NAICS (North American Industry Classification System) codes, as opposed to the SIC (Standard Industrial Classification) codes.

3. **UDDI green pages:** information about a company's key business processes, such as operating platform, supported programs, purchasing meth-

ods, shipping and billing requirements, and other higher-level business protocols.

For an example of how UDDI is used in Web Services, see page 23.

Web Services Description Language (WSDL)

WSDL is a format for describing a Web Services interface. It is a way to describe services and how they should be bound to specific network addresses. WSDL has three parts:

1. Definitions
2. Operations
3. Service bindings

Definitions are generally expressed in XML and include both data type definitions and message definitions that use the data type definitions. These definitions are usually based upon some agreed upon XML vocabulary. This agreement could be within an organization or between organizations. Vocabularies within an organization could be designed specifically for that organization. They may or may not be based on some industry-wide vocabulary. If data type and message definitions need to be used between organizations, then most likely an industry-wide vocabulary will be used. For more on XML vocabularies, see page 212.

XML, however, is not required for definitions. The OMG Interface Definition Language (IDL), for example, could be used instead of XML. If a different definitional format were used, senders and receivers would need to agree on the format as well as the vocabulary. Nevertheless, over time, XML-based vocabularies and messages are likely to dominate.

Operations describe actions for the messages supported by a Web service. There are four types of operations:

1. **One-way:** Messages sent without a reply required
2. **Request/response:** The sender sends a message and the receiver sends a reply.
3. **Solicit response:** A request for a response. (The specific definition for this action is pending.)
4. **Notification:** Messages sent to multiple receivers. (The specific definition for this action is pending.)

Operations are grouped into port types. Port types define a set of operations supported by the Web service.

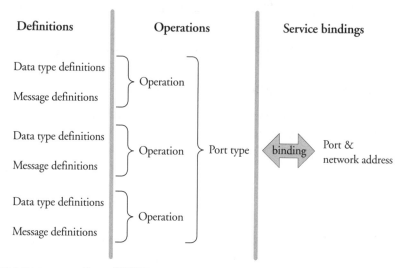

FIGURE 14.2 Parts of WSDL.

Service bindings connect port types to a port. A port is defined by associating a network address with a port type. A collection of ports defines a service. This binding is commonly created using SOAP, but other forms may be used. These other forms could include CORBA Internet Inter-ORB Protocol (IIOP), DCOM, .NET, Java Message Service (JMS), or WebSphere MQ (formerly MQSeries) to name a few.

XML Namespaces are used to ensure uniqueness of the XML element names in the definitions, operations, and service bindings.

Figure 14.2 shows the relationship of the basic parts of WSDL. For an example of how WSDL is used in Web Services, see page 22.

ebXML Registry

The ebXML Registry is similar to UDDI in that it allows businesses to find one another, to define trading-partner agreements, and to exchange XML messages in support of business operations. The goal is to allow all these activities to be performed automatically, without human intervention, over the Internet. The ebXML architecture has many similarities to SOAP/WSDL/ UDDI, and some convergence is taking place with the adoption of SOAP in the ebXML transport specification. RosettaNet also announced its adoption of the ebXML transport. The ebXML messaging specification is based on SOAP with Attachments, but does not use WSDL. ebXML does add security, guaranteed messaging, and compliance with business process interaction specifications.

The ebXML initiative is sponsored by the United Nations Centre for Trade Facilitation and Electronic Business (UN/CEFACT) and OASIS to research, develop, and promote global standards for the use of XML to facilitate the exchange of electronic business data. A major goal for ebXML is to produce standards that serve the same or similar purpose as EDI, including support for emerging industry-specific XML vocabularies. ebXML and Web Services hold the promise of realizing the original goals of EDI, making it simpler and easier to exchange electronic documents over the Internet. See page 65 for a discussion of why this is simpler.

XML Specifications

XML shares common origins with HTML and SGML. SGML or "Standard Generalized Markup Language" was issued as an international standard (ISO 8879) in 1986. It was intended for semantic markup that would assist computer cataloging and indexing. SGML provided flexibility that had not been available before. It was, however, very complex.

About 1990, Tim Berners-Lee at CERN developed a new, simpler language that could be used in place of SGML. Thus, HTML or "Hyper-Text Markup Language" was intended to be a simpler language that did not require expensive authoring tools. HTML succeeded beyond anyone's expectations but it lacked a certain flexibility that developers wanted. Various groups made changes and added extensions until HTML's roots had been mangled.

In the summer of 1996, a working group at W3C was formed to create a markup language that would combine the strength of SGML with the simplicity of HTML. The first official draft specification for XML was released in November 1996. XML version 1.0 became a W3C recommendation in 1998.

The basic structure of XML is the document. This terminology, however, might cause one to think of XML as only a richer, more flexible HTML. It is richer and more flexible, but it can be so much more as well.

Thinking of XML as a document allows you to see how it can be used for presentation of data. This presentation can be detailed and useful as we will see from the way XML is constructed.

XML does, however, actually go beyond documents. It can be used for the communication of data as well. XML uses a flexible tagged structure that makes it more robust than a fixed record format for communication. This is how many Web Services specifications use XML.

Finally, XML can also be used to define the storage of data. The same flexible tagged structure can be used when storing data. This is how some database management products use XML.

This section provides a brief background on many of the relevant XML specifications.

XML Schema

XML Schemas express shared vocabularies and allow machines to carry out rules made by people. They provide a means for defining the structure, content, and semantics of XML documents.

REgular LAnguage description for XML (RELAX)

REgular LAnguage description for XML (RELAX) is a specification for describing XML-based languages. It is standardized by INSTAC XML SWG of Japan. Under the auspices of the Japanese Standard Association (JSA), this committee develops Japanese national standards for XML. See RELAX NG.

RELAX NG

The purpose of this committee is to create a specification for a schema language for XML based on TREX and RELAX. The key features of RELAX NG are that it does not change the information set of an XML document, and supports XML Namespaces, unordered content, and mixed content.

Tree Regular Expressions for XML (TREX)

Tree Regular Expressions for XML (TREX) is a language for validating XML documents. TREX has been merged with RELAX to create RELAX NG. All future development of TREX will take place as part of the RELAX NG effort. See RELAX NG.

Schematron

The Schematron is a language and toolkit for making assertions about patterns found in XML documents. It can be used as a friendly validation language and for automatically generating external annotation (links, RDF, perhaps Topic Maps). Because it uses paths rather than grammars, it can be used to assert constraints that cannot be expressed using XML Schemas. Schematron was developed at the Academia Sinica Computing Centre, ASCC.

eXtensible Stylesheet Language (XSL)

eXtensible Stylesheet Language (XSL) is a language for expressing stylesheets. It consists of three parts: XSL Transformations (XSLT): a language for transforming XML documents, the XML Path Language (XPath), an expression language used by XSLT to access or refer to parts of an XML document. (XPath is also used by the XLink specification). The third part is XSL Formatting Objects (XSL-FO): an XML vocabulary for specifying formatting semantics. An XSL stylesheet specifies the presentation of a class of XML documents by describing how an instance of the class is transformed into an XML document that uses the formatting vocabulary.

XSL Formatting Objects (XSL-FO)

XSL Formatting Objects (XSL-FO), is a set of tools developers and Web designers use to specify the vocabulary and semantics for paginated presentation.

XML Linking Language (XLink)

XML Linking Language (XLink) allows elements to be inserted into XML documents to create and describe links between resources. It uses XML syntax to create structures that can describe the simple unidirectional hyperlinks of HTML, as well as more sophisticated links.

XML Namespaces

An XML namespace is a collection of names, identified by a URI, which are used in XML documents as element types and attribute names. XML Namespaces differ from the "namespaces" conventionally used in computing disciplines in that the XML version has internal structure and is not, mathematically speaking, a set.

XML Path Language (XPath)

XML Path Language (XPath) is the result of an effort to provide a common syntax and semantics for functionality shared between XSL Transformations and XPointer. The primary purpose of XPath is to address parts of an XML document.

XML Pointer Language (XPointer)

XML Pointer Language (XPointer) allows addressing the internal structures of XML documents. It allows for examination of a hierarchical document structure and choice of its internal parts based on various properties, such as element types, attribute values, character content, and relative position.

XML Signature

XML Signature is an XML syntax used for representing signatures on digital content and procedures for computing and verifying such signatures. Signatures provide for data integrity and authentication.

XSL Transformations (XSLT)

XSL Transformations (XSLT) is a language for transforming XML documents into other XML documents. XSLT is designed for use as part of XSL, which is a stylesheet language for XML. In addition to XSLT, XSL includes an XML vocabulary for specifying formatting. XSL specifies the styling of an XML document by using XSLT to describe how the document is transformed into another XML document that uses the formatting vocabulary. XSLT may be used independently of XSL. However, XSLT is not intended as a completely general-purpose XML transformation language. Rather it is designed primarily for the kinds of transformations that are needed when XSLT is used as part of XSL.

XQuery

XQuery is designed to be a language in which queries are concise and easily understood. It is also flexible enough to query a broad spectrum of XML information sources, including both databases and documents.

XML Vocabularies

Every industry group has its own vocabulary for its activity. Various industry groups have been developing the XML version of their respective vocabularies to take advantage of the XML messaging capability of Web Services. This is XML used in the messages defined used by WSDL and sent using SOAP or other protocols.

First, an important development in XML vocabularies will be covered. This is the Universal Business Language (UBL). Then a sampling of vocabularies is listed. By no means are all vocabularies listed here. This is meant to give a taste of all the work being done right now on XML vocabularies. The organizations working on each vocabulary is shown in italics at the end of the description.

This is a dynamic area for Web Services. For an updated listing, go to www.service-architecture.com. Links for each of these vocabularies can also be found at that Web site.

Universal Business Language (UBL)

The Universal Business Language (UBL) in OASIS is an important development in the use of XML vocabularies. In any human language, the same word can mean different things for different industries. Conversely, different words sometimes can mean the same thing in different industries. The OASIS UBL Technical Committee's charter is to define a common XML business document library. UBL will provide a set of XML building blocks and a framework that will enable trading partners to unambiguously identify and exchange business documents in specific contexts. This is an effort to unite efforts underway by organizations and standards groups around the world. The OASIS UBL Technical Committee intends to enhance and harmonize overlapping XML business libraries and similar technologies to advance consensus on an international standard. *OASIS*

Accounting

Small and medium-sized business XML (smbXML): XML specification for describing business transactions. smbXML is specifically designed for the needs of the small to medium-sized business community. *NetLedger/Oracle*

Astronomy

The Astronomical Instrument Markup Language (AIML): XML specification for the command and control astronomical instruments (e.g., telescopes, cameras, and spectrometers). Based on IML. *NASA*

Flexible Image Transport System Markup Language (FITSML): XML specification for astronomical data, such as images, spectra, tables, and sky atlases. Based on the XDF. *Goddard Space Flight Center/NASA*

Chemistry

Chem eStandards: XML specification for data exchange developed specifically for the buying, selling, and delivery of chemicals. *Chemistry Industry Data eXchange (CIDX)*

Chemical Markup Language (CML): XML specification covering macromolecular sequences to inorganic molecules and quantum chemistry. *xml-cml.org*

Construction

Architecture Description Markup Language (ADML): XML specification for architecture. ADML is based on ACME, an architecture description language. ADML adds to ACME a standardized representation the ability to define links to objects outside the architecture (such as rationale, designs, and components). *The Open Group*

Customer Information

eXtensible Name Address Language (xNAL): XML specification for managing name and address data regardless of country of origin. It consists of two parts: xNL: eXtensible Name Language to define the name components, and xAL: eXtensible Address Language to define the address components. *OASIS*

Education

Schools Interoperability Framework (SIF): XML specification for ensuring that K-12 instructional and administrative software applications work together more effectively. *Software & Information Industry Association*

XML/Electronic Data Interchange (EDI)

XML/Electronic Data Interchange (EDI): XML specification to exchange different types of data (e.g., an invoice, healthcare claim, or project status). It includes implementing EDI dictionaries and on-line repositories to business language, rules, and objects. *XML/EDI Group*

Finance

eXtensible Business Reporting Language (XBRL): XML specification that describes financial information for public and private companies and other organizations. *xbrl.org*

Financial Information eXchange (FIX): XML specification for the real-time electronic exchange of securities transactions. *FIX Protocol*

Financial products Markup Language (FpML): XML specification for swaps, derivatives, and structured financial products. *fpml.org*

Interactive Financial Exchange (IFX): XML specification for electronic bill presentment and payment, business to business payments, business to business banking (such as balance and transaction reporting, remittance information), automated teller machine communications, consumer to business payments, and consumer to business banking. *IFX Forum*

Government

Election Markup Language (EML): XML specification for the structured interchange of data among hardware, software, and service providers who engage in any aspect of providing election or voter services to public or private organizations. The services performed for such elections include but are not limited to voter roll/membership maintenance (new voter registration, membership and dues collection, change of address tracking, etc.), citizen/membership credentialing, redistricting, requests for absentee/expatriate ballots, election calendaring, logistics management (polling place management), election notification, ballot delivery and tabulation, election results reporting, and demographics. *OASIS*

Healthcare

Health Level 7 (HL7) Healthcare XML Format: XML specification for the exchange of clinical data and information. The purpose of the exchange of clinical data includes, but is not limited to: provision of clinical care, support of clinical and administrative research, execution of automated transaction oriented decision logic (medical logic modules), support of outcomes research, support of clinical trials, and to support data reporting to government and other authorized third parties. *Health Level Seven*

Human Resources

HR-XML: XML specification designed to enable e-business and the automation of human resources-related data exchanges. *HR-XML Consortium*

Insurance

ACORD XML for Life Insurance: XML specification based on the ACORD Life Data Model. *ACORD*

ACORD XML for Property and Casualty Insurance: XML specification that addresses the real-time requirement by defining property and casualty transactions that include both request and response messages for personal lines, commercial lines, specialty lines, surety, claims, and accounting transactions. *ACORD*

Instruments

Instrument Markup Language (IML): XML specification that applies to virtually any kind of instrument that can be controlled by a computer. The approach to instrument description and control apply to many domains, from medical instruments (e.g., microscopes) to printing presses to machine assembly lines. The concepts behind IML apply equally well to the description and control of instruments in general. *NASA*

Legal

LegalXML has many subcategories of specifications. They are shown below. *OASIS*

LegalXML Electronic Court Filing: specifications for the use of XML to create legal documents and to transmit legal documents from an attorney, party or self-represented litigant to a court, from a court to an attorney, party or self-represented litigant or to another court, and from an attorney or other user to another attorney or other user of legal documents.

LegalXML eContracts: open XML standards for the markup of contract documents to enable the efficient creation, maintenance, management, exchange, and publication of contract documents and contract terms.

LegalXML eNotary: an agreed set of technical requirements to govern self-proving electronic legal information.

LegalXML Integrated Justice: XML specifications for exchanging data among justice system branches and agencies.

LegalXML Legislative Documents: XML standards for the markup of legislative documents and a system of simple citation capability for non-legislative documents (e.g., newspaper articles). The primary goal is to allow the public to more easily participate in the democratic process by creating a more open, accessible, easier to parse, research, and reference legislative documents.

LegalXML Legal Transcripts: XML syntax for representing legal transcript documents either as stand-alone structured content or as part of other legal records.

Math

MathML: XML specification for describing mathematical notation and capturing both its structure and content. The goal of MathML is to enable mathematics to be served, received, and processed on the Internet, just as HTML has enabled this functionality for text. *W3C*

OpenMath: XML specification for representing mathematical objects with their semantics, allowing them to be exchanged between computer programs, stored in databases, or published on the worldwide Web. There is a strong relationship to the MathML recommendation from the Worldwide Web Consortium, and a large overlap between the two developer communities. MathML deals principally with the presentation of mathematical objects, while OpenMath is solely concerned with their semantic meaning or content. While MathML does have some limited facilities for dealing with content, it also allows semantic information encoded in OpenMath to be embedded inside a MathML structure. Thus, the two specifications may be seen as complementary. *The OpenMath Society*

Open Mathematical Documents (OMDoc): XML specification for repre-senting the semantics and structure of various kinds of mathematical docu-ments, including articles, textbooks, interactive books, courses. OMDoc is an extension of the OpenMath and MathML standards, and in particular of the content part of MathML. *mathweb.org*

eXtensible Data Format (XDF): XML specification for general mathe-matical principles that can be used throughout the scientific disciplines. *Astronomical Data Center (ADC) at Goddard Space Flight Center/NASA*

News

News Industry Text Format (NITF): XML specification for the content and structure of news articles. *International Press Telecommunications Council*

Publishing Requirements for Industry Standard Markup (PRISM): XML specification for syndicating, aggregating, post-processing and multi-purposing content from magazines, news, catalogs, books, and mainstream journals. *IDEAlliance*

Physics

Common Data Format Markup Language (CDFML): XML specification that is a self-describing data abstraction for the storage and manipulation of multi-dimensional data in a discipline-independent fashion. One of the CDFML's goals is, as a proof of concept, demonstrating the interoperability between CDF and Flexible Image Transport System (see FTSML) using XDF as the intermediary format. *National Space Science Data Center's (NSSDC)*

Real Estate

Mortgage Industry Standards Maintenance Organization (MISMO): XML specification for commercial mortgage origination data that provides both the content and format for borrowers and mortgage bankers to transmit data to lenders. *Mortgage Industry Standards Maintenance Organization*

Real Estate Transaction Markup Language (RETML): XML specification for exchanging real estate transaction information. *rets-wg.org*

Telecommunications

Telecommunications Interchange Markup (TIM): XML specification for describing the structure of telecommunications and other technical documents. *Alliance for Telecommunications Industry Solutions (ATIS)*

Travel

The OpenTravel Alliance (OTA): XML specification that serves as a common language for travel-related terminology and a mechanism for promoting the exchange of information across all travel industry segments. *OpenTravel Alliance*

CHAPTER 15

Quick Reference Guide

This chapter serves as a quick reference to various technologies and concepts related to service-oriented architectures. For those entries that have related examples or more information in this book, there is a reference at the end where you can find the additional information.

Because Web Services is a dynamic area, new and revised technologies and concepts will be occurring regularly. If you cannot find what you need in this guide or to get an updated reference list, go to www.service-architecture .com.

Adapters

The adapters allow Web Services connections with internally developed systems or packaged software. There can also be adapters between Web Services and CORBA or DCOM. For examples, see page 53.

Agents

Agents are active entities that work with Web Services. On a relatively simple side, there are agents that can help us shop online. More sophisticated agents would be able to perform negotiations, monitor the status of systems, or monitor changes in the content of databases or other systems. These agents could communicate with each other using Web Services or they could communicate with other systems internal or external to the organization using Web Services. For examples, see page 164.

Application Server

An application server is a component-based product that resides in the middle-tier of an architecture. It provides middleware services for security and state maintenance, along with data access and persistence. The two commercial categories of applications servers are Java applications servers based on J2EE or subsequent specifications or Microsoft's .NET. For more discussion, see page 167.

Business Intelligence (BI)

Business intelligence (BI) software is a broad area covering data mining, pattern finding, reporting, and event detection among other possible functions. Often, BI is used with data marts and data warehouses, but that is not a mandatory requirement. For more discussion, see page 162.

Business Objects

Business objects are a way of representing something in the business domain, including various attributes, behavior, relationships, and constraints. They are usually used in the middle tier of a multi-tier architecture. For more discussion of a middle-tier architecture, see page 167.

Business Process Execution Language for Web Services (BPEL4WS)

Business Process Execution Language for Web Services (BPEL4WS) defines a notation for specifying business process behavior based on Web Services. Business processes can be described in two ways:

1. Executable business processes model actual behavior of a participant in a business interaction.

2. Business protocols, in contrast, use process descriptions that specify the mutually visible message exchange behavior of each of the parties involved in the protocol, without revealing their internal behavior. The process descriptions for business protocols are called abstract processes.

BPEL4WS is used to model the behavior of both executable and abstract processes.

Business Process Modeling Language (BPML)

The Business Process Modeling Language (BPML) is a meta-language for the modeling of business processes, just as XML is a meta-language for the modeling of business data. BPML provides an abstracted execution model for collaborative and transactional business processes based on the concept of a transactional finite-state machine.

Business Process Query Language (BPQL)

The Business Process Query Language (BPQL) is a management interface to a business process management infrastructure that includes a process execution facility (process server) and a process deployment facility (process repository).

Business Process Specification Schema (BPSS)

The Business Process Specification Schema (BPSS) is a standard framework by which business systems may be configured to support execution of business collaborations consisting of business transactions. It is based upon prior UN/CEFACT work, specifically the meta-model behind the UN/CEFACT Modeling Methodology (UMM) defined in the N090R9.1 specification. The specification schema supports the specification of business transactions and the choreography of business transactions into business collaborations. These patterns determine the actual exchange of business documents and business signals between the partners to achieve the required electronic commerce transaction.

Cache Synchronization

Cache synchronization refers to keeping the data values in cache synchronized with the data values in the underlying database. For an example, see page 172.

Caching

Caching is the retention of data to minimize network traffic flow and/or disk access. For more discussion, see page 169.

Collaboration Protocol Profile/Agreement (CPP/A)

Collaboration Protocol Profile/Agreement (CPP/A) provides interoperability between two parties even though they may use application software and runtime support software from different vendors. The Collaboration Protocol

Profile (CPP) defines message-exchange capabilities and the business collaborations that it supports. The Collaboration Protocol Agreement (CPA) defines the way two parties will interact in performing the chosen business collaboration.

Common Warehouse Meta-model (CWM)

The Common Warehouse Meta-model (CWM) provides standard interfaces that can be used to enable easy interchange of warehouse and business intelligence metadata between warehouse tools, warehouse platforms, and warehouse metadata repositories in distributed heterogeneous environments.

Composite Application

A composite application is created by combining services. Composite applications are built using a service-oriented architecture.

CORBA

CORBA is the acronym for Common Object Request Broker Architecture. It was developed under the auspices of the Object Management Group (OMG). It is middleware. A CORBA-based program from any vendor, on almost any computer, operating system, programming language, and network, can interoperate with a CORBA-based program from the same or another vendor, on almost any other computer, operating system, programming language, and network.

The first service-oriented architecture for many people in the past was with the use of Object Request Brokers (ORBs) based on the CORBA specification. The CORBA specification is responsible for really increasing the awareness of service-oriented architectures. For more discussion, see page 45.

Data Cleansing

Data cleansing are changes made to improve data quality. For existing data being loaded into a data mart or data warehouse, ETL software could be used to improve the quality of the data. For more discussion, see page 52.

Data Mart

A data mart is a database, or collection of databases, often found at the department level of an organization. Sometimes they are designed for a particular subject or subset of data. It is possible for a collection of data marts to form the basis of a data warehouse. The development of data warehouses may involve extract, transform, and load (ETL) software. For more discussion, see pages 50 and 162.

Data Warehouse

A data warehouse often refers to combining data from many different sources across an enterprise. It is also referred to as enterprise data warehouse (EDW). The development of data warehouses usually involves extract, transform, and load (ETL) software. For more discussion, see pages 50 and 162.

DCOM

DCOM is the acronym for the Distributed Component Object Model, an extension of the Component Object Model (COM). DCOM was introduced in 1996 and is designed for use across multiple network transports, including Internet protocols such as HTTP. DCOM is based on the Open Software Foundation's DCE-RPC spec and will work with both Java applets and ActiveX components through its use of the Component Object Model (COM). It works primarily with Microsoft Windows. For more discussion, see page 45.

Directory

A directory is a network service that identifies resources on a network and makes them accessible to users and applications. For Web Services, directories could use UDDI or the ebXML directory. For an example, see page 22.

Enterprise JavaBeans (EJB)

Enterprise JavaBeans (EJBs) manage and coordinate the allocation of resources to the applications. Enterprise beans typically contain the business logic for a Java application. The EJB server must provide one or more EJB containers. An EJB container manages the enterprise beans contained within it. For each enterprise bean, the container is responsible for registering the object, providing a remote interface for the object, creating and destroying object instances, checking security for the object, managing the active state of the object, and coordinating distributed transactions. Optionally, the container can also manage all persistent data within the object. Also, see Java application servers in this guide.

Electronic Data Interchange (EDI)

Electronic Data Interchange (EDI) began as early as the late 1960s. Over the years, there have been significant efforts on standards for EDI. Two significant standards efforts are in the INCITS (ANSI) ASC X12 committee and UN/ EDIFACT (United Nations/Electronic Data Interchange For Administration, Commerce and Transport.) These standards groups are also working with the ebXML and RosettaNet groups. For more discussion, see page 65.

eXtensible Access Control Markup Language (XACML)

The Extensible Access Control Markup Language (XACML) provides fine grained control of authorized activities, the effect of characteristics of the access requestor, the protocol over which the request is made, authorization based on classes of activities, and content introspection.

eXtensible rights Markup Language (XrML)

eXtensible rights Markup Language (XrML) is a digital rights language designed for securely specifying and managing rights and conditions associated with various resources including digital content as well as services.

Extract, Transform, and Load (ETL)

Extract, transform, and load (ETL) products are used to migrate data from one source to some destination. The destination is usually a database. The source can be a database or most any other source. The "extract" part is to select data from the source. "Transform" reformats and possibly corrects the extracted data. "Load" places the transformed data into the destination database. Also, see data warehouse and data mart in this guide. For more discussion, see page 50.

Failover

Failover is the process of a secondary machine taking over for a primary machine. For database failover, see replication in this guide. For more discussion, see page 142.

Gadget

Gadgets are components that can be added to a Web site to provide dynamic content. For more discussion, see page 62.

HTTP

HTTP stands for HyperText Transfer Protocol. It is a mechanism for sending requests and responses between computers connected to the Internet or an Intranet. For more discussion on HTTP and SOAP, see page 205.

Internet Inter-ORB Protocol (IIOP)

The Internet Inter-ORB Protocol (IIOP) is the protocol used for communication between CORBA object request brokers (ORBs). Also, see CORBA in this guide.

J2EE

See Java application servers in this guide.

Java API for XML Parsing (JAXP)

The Java API for XML Parsing (JAXP) allows developers to easily use XML Parsers in their applications.

Java Application Servers

Java application servers are based on the Java 2 Platform, Enterprise Edition (J2EE). J2EE uses a multi-tier distributed model. The J2EE Platform consists of a Web Server and an EJB Server. (These servers are also called "containers.") The Web container provides the runtime environment through components that provide naming context and life cycle management. Some Web servers may also provide additional services such as security and concurrency control. A Web server may work with an EJB server to provide some of those services. A Web server, however, does not need to be located on the same machine as an EJB server. The EJB server provides an environment that supports the execution of applications developed using Enterprise JavaBeans (EJB) components. It manages and coordinates the allocation of resources to the applications. Enterprise beans typically contain the business logic for a J2EE application. Also, see EJB in this guide. More discussion can be found on page 167.

Load Leveling

Load leveling is a design strategy that spreads activity or load across more than one machine. For examples, see page 140.

Mapping

Mapping is the technique used to make one or more rows in database tables appear as programming language objects or XML. For more discussion, see www.service-architecture.com.

Message Router

Message routers direct data from a requesting resource to a responding resource and back. These are also known as application brokers or message brokers. A router "knows" which of the other internal systems needs to receive a certain type of updates. The individual internal systems can pass updates to a router and would not need to know who receives such updates. A message router usually needs to transform the data in some way in order to match the format of the data expected by the receiving system. For more discussion, see page 52.

Message Service Specification (MSS)

Message Service Specification (MSS) is a communications-protocol neutral method for exchanging electronic business messages. It supports reliable, secure delivery of business information and a flexible enveloping technique, permitting messages of any format type.

Meta-Object Facility (MOF)

The Meta-Object Facility (MOF) is a set of standard interfaces that can be used to define and manipulate a set of interoperable meta-models and their corresponding models.

Middleware

Middleware hides the complexity of the communication between two or more systems or services. This simplifies the development of those systems and services and isolates the complexity of the communication between them. The different systems or services can be on the same hardware or on different hardware. For more discussion, see page 43.

Model Driven Architecture (MDA)

The Model Driven Architecture (MDA) is an open, vendor-neutral approach to interoperability using OMG's modeling specifications: Unified Modeling

Language (UML), Meta-Object Facility (MOF), and Common Warehouse Meta-model (CWM).

.NET

Microsoft .NET is a set of Microsoft software technologies for Web Services. Microsoft .NET is made up of three core components:

1. .NET building block services
2. .NET device software for devices such as mobile phones, pagers, and so on
3. .NET infrastructure, which includes:
   - .NET Framework—the Common Language Runtime (CLR) and .NET Framework class libraries
   - Microsoft Visual Studio.NET: Visual Basic .NET, Visual C# .NET, Visual C++ .NET, Visual FoxPro, and so on
   - Servers called .NET Enterprise Servers

More discussion can be found on page 167.

Object Request Broker (ORB)

The Object Request Broker (ORB) is middleware that uses the CORBA specification. Also see CORBA in this guide.

OMG Interface Definition Language (IDL)

The OMG Interface Definition Language (IDL) permits interfaces to objects to be defined independent of an object's implementation. After defining an interface in IDL, the interface definition is used as input to an IDL compiler that produces output to be compiled and linked with an object implementation and its clients. Also see CORBA in this guide. (There are other uses of the IDL initialisms. For example, there is also a Java IDL.)

Partner Interface Process (PIP)

A Partner Interface Process (PIP) defines business processes between trading partners. PIPs fit into seven clusters, or groups of core business processes, that represent the backbone of the trading network. Each cluster is broken down into segments—cross-enterprise processes involving more than one type of trading partner. Within each Segment are individual PIPs. PIPs are specialized system-to-system XML-based dialogs. Each PIP specification includes a business document with the vocabulary, and a business process with the choreography of the message dialog.

Replication

Replication is the process of making multiple copies of data on separate machines. The replicated data will be available on the secondary machine should it need to take over when the primary machine fails. See failover in this guide. For more discussion, see page 143.

Resource Description Framework (RDF)

Resource Description Framework (RDF) is a way of describing a Web site's metadata, or the data about the data at the site.

RosettaNet Implementation Framework (RNIF)

The RosettaNet Implementation Framework (RNIF) provides the packaging, routing, and transport of RosettaNet PIP messages and business signals.

Security Assertion Markup Language (SAML)

The Security Assertion Markup Language (SAML) is an XML framework for exchanging authentication and authorization information.

Service

A service is a function that is well-defined, self-contained, and does not depend on the context or state of other services. For more discussion, see page 19.

Service Provisioning Markup Language (SPML)

Service Provisioning Markup Language (SPML) is an XML-based framework specification for exchanging user, resource, and service provisioning information. The SPML specification is being developed with consideration of the following provisioning-related specifications: Active Digital Profile (ADPr), eXtensible Resource Provisioning Management (XRPM), and Information Technology Markup Language (ITML).

Service-Oriented Architecture

A service-oriented architecture is essentially a collection of services. These services communicate with each other. The communication can involve either simple data passing or it could involve two or more services coordinating some activity. For more discussion, see page 18.

Unified Modeling Language (UML)

The Unified Modeling Language (UML) is a specification of a graphical language used for visualizing, specifying, constructing, and documenting the artifacts of distributed object systems.

Uniform Resource Identifier (URI)

Uniform Resource Identifiers (URIs, also known as URLs) are short strings that identify resources in the Web: documents, images, downloadable files, services, electronic mailboxes, and other resources.

Universal Data Model

A universal data model is a template or generic data model that can be used as a building block for the development of a data model. For more discussion, see page 120.

Web Distributed Data Exchange (WDDX)

Web Distributed Data Exchange (WDDX) is an XML-based technology that enables the exchange of complex data between Web programming languages. WDDX consists of a language-independent representation of data based on XML, and a set of modules for a wide variety of languages that use WDDX.

Web Services Endpoint Language (WSEL)

The Web Services Endpoint Language (WSEL) is an XML format for the description of non-operational characteristics of service endpoints, like quality-of-service, cost, or security properties.

Web Services Component Model

The Web Services Component Model is an XML and Web Services centric component model for interactive Web applications. The designs must achieve two main goals: enable businesses to distribute Web applications through multiple revenue channels, and enable new services or applications to be created by leveraging existing applications across the Web.

Web Services Conversation Language (WSCL)

Web Services Conversation Language (WSCL) allows the business level conversations or public processes supported by a Web service to be defined. WSCL specifies the XML documents being exchanged, and the allowed sequencing of these document exchanges. WSCL conversation definitions are themselves XML documents and can therefore be interpreted by Web Services infrastructures and development tools.

Web Services Experience Language (WSXL)

Web Services Experience Language (WSXL) enables businesses to distribute Web applications through multiple revenue channels and to enable new services or applications to be created by leveraging existing applications across the Web. WSXL is built on widely accepted established and emerging open standards, and is designed to be independent of execution platform, browser, and presentation markup. Interactive Web applications that are developed using WSXL can be delivered to end users through a diversity of deployment channels: directly to a browser, indirectly through a portal, or by embedding into a third party Web application.

Web Services Flow Language (WSFL)

Web Services Flow Language (WSFL) is a language for the description of Web Services compositions. WSFL considers two types of Web Services compositions:

1. The appropriate usage pattern of a collection of Web Services, in such a way that the resulting composition describes how to achieve a particular business goal; typically, the result is a description of a business process

2. The interaction pattern of a collection of Web Services; in this case, the result is a description of the overall partner interactions

Web Services for Interactive Applications (WSIA)

Web Services for Interactive Applications (WSIA) is an XML and Web Services centric framework for interactive Web applications. The designs must achieve two main goals: enable businesses to distribute Web applications through multiple revenue channels, and enable new services or applications to be created by leveraging existing applications across the Web.

Web Services for Remote Portals (WSRP)

Web Services for Remote Portals (WSRP) is an XML and Web Services standard that will allow for the plug-n-play of: portals, other intermediary Web applications that aggregate content, and applications from disparate sources. These Web Services for Remote Portals will be designed to enable businesses to provide content or applications in a form that does not require any manual content or application-specific adaptation by consuming applications.

Web Services User Interface (WSUI)

Web Services User Interface (WSUI) enables Web platforms implemented in entirely different languages (Java, COM/.NET, and Perl) to interoperate and share applications. By using WSUI, an application can be packaged with a WSUI descriptor file and an XSLT stylesheet and be dynamically integrated into another Web site that is running a WSUI container implementation.

XLANG

XLANG is a notation for the automation of business processes based on Web Services for the specification of message exchange behavior among participating Web Services. XLANG is expected to serve as the basis for automated protocol engines that can track the state of process instances and help enforce protocol correctness in message flows.

XML Common Biometric Format (XCBF)

XML Common Biometric Format (XCBF) is a common set of secure XML encoding for the formats specified in CBEFF, the Common Biometric Exchange File Format.

XML Encryption

XML Encryption is a process for encrypting/decrypting digital content (including XML documents and portions thereof) and an XML syntax used to represent the encrypted content and information that enables an intended recipient to decrypt it.

XML Key Management Specification (XKMS)

The XML Key Management Specification (XKMS) is a specification of XML application/protocol that allows a simple client to obtain key information (values, certificates, and management or trust data) from a Web service.

XML Protocol (XMLP)

XML Protocol (XMLP) provides simple protocols that can be ubiquitously deployed and easily programmed through scripting languages, XML tools, interactive Web development tools, etc. The goal is a layered system which will directly meet the needs of applications with simple interfaces (e.g., get-StockQuote, validateCreditCard), and which can be incrementally extended to provide the security, scalability, and robustness required for more complex application interfaces.

XML Signature

XML Signature is an XML syntax used for representing signatures on digital content and procedures for computing and verifying such signatures. Signatures provide for data integrity and authentication.

Index